In the Strength
of the Lord
I Can Do All
Things

Carolyn J. Rasmus

In the Strength
of the Lord
I Can Do All
Things

Deseret Book Company
Salt Lake City, Utah

*To my "goodly parents," who taught
me to "walk uprightly before the
Lord" (D&C 68:28), and to my
many friends who are an "example
of the believers, in word, in
conversation, in charity, in spirit, in
faith, in purity" (1 Timothy 3:12).*

©1990 Deseret Book Company

Library of Congress Cataloging-in-Publication Data

Rasmus, Carolyn J.
In the strength of the Lord I can do all things / by Carolyn J.
   Rasmus.
    p.   cm.
1. Spiritual life—Mormon authors.   I. Title.
BX8656.R37   1990
248.4'893—dc20   89-78380
                                                                CIP

Printed in the United States of America
10   9   8   7   6   5   4   3   2   1

Contents

Preface

Putting thoughts and ideas and feelings into written words is never easy, especially when writing about things of the Spirit. Nephi stated that he was not "mighty in writing, like unto speaking," and explained that "when a man speaketh by the power of the Holy Ghost the power of the Holy Ghost carrieth it unto the hearts of the children of men." (2 Nephi 33:1.) Likewise, the prophet Ether expressed concern to the Lord about his writings, fearing that the readers would "mock these things, because of our weakness in writing." He, too, acknowledged that the Lord "made us mighty in word . . . because of the Holy Ghost," and complained that "when we write we behold our weakness, and stumble because of the placing of our words." He was fearful that those who read their writings would "mock at our words." (Ether 12:23.)

It was then that the Lord taught Ether a powerful lesson, a lesson which I believe applies not only to those who attempt to write, but to all who feel inadequate, unprepared, and unequal to a task: "And if men come unto me I will show unto them their weakness. I give unto men weakness that they may be humble; and my grace is sufficient for all men that humble themselves before me; for if they humble themselves before me, and have faith in me, then will I make weak things become strong unto them." (Ether 12:27.)

If this book contains thoughts or ideas which are helpful to the reader, may it serve as evidence that his grace is indeed sufficient and that each of us can, "in the strength of the Lord," accomplish many things which are beyond our natural abilities.

Try the Virtue of the Word of God

Frequently I am asked to talk about the events that led to my conversion. I am always eager to share my experiences for the same reasons that others, especially those in the Book of Mormon, related their conversion experiences—that it might "cause great joy" (Alma 27:26), and that those who hear my testimony may know "there is no other way or means whereby man can be saved, only in and through Christ" (Alma 38:9). I also believe strongly that the conversion process is just that—a process. Although we have several recorded incidents of people who experienced a miraculous event in their lives and who were "converted" immediately, such as Saul and Alma the Younger (see Acts 9:1–22 and Mosiah 27:13–32), most of us come to a knowledge of the truth in just the way the Lord tells us we will: "I will give unto the children of men line upon line, precept upon precept, here a little and there a little" (2 Nephi 28:30; see also D&C 98:12; 128:21).

The process of my conversion began at a very early age. Like Nephi, I was "born of goodly parents." (1 Nephi 1:1.) I attended weekly Church services with my parents who, for as long as I can remember, either taught Sunday School or served in leadership positions in our community Lutheran Church. One of the most used books in our home was *Hurlbut's Story of the Bible for Young and Old.* I remember being read to from this book and recall studying the many pictures and illustrations. I loved the titles of the stories, "The First Baby in the World, and His Brother," "Jacob's Wonderful Dream," "The Promise of the Woman of Shunem," and many, many more.

I can also vividly recall a sunny, summer day when I was about four years old. My mother was hanging clothes on the clothesline and I was swinging so high I was sure I'd go over the top and around the swing. At the top of my lungs I was singing, "Jesus Wants Me for a Sunbeam." At that moment I knew as surely as I would ever know that, as Robert Browning said, "God's in his heaven, All's right with the world!"

Following the example set by my parents, I found myself involved in teaching Sunday School and singing in the church choir during my college years and later as I taught in New York and Iowa. Most of my close friends, wherever I lived, were also Christians — people who were "doers of the word, and not hearers only." (James 1:22.)

While involved in a professional organization I became acquainted with Dr. Leona Holbrook, a professor at Brigham Young University and then president of the American Association for Health, Physical Education, and Recreation. Each time I heard her speak I was impressed not only with what she said, but the manner with which she spoke. But more significantly, I was touched as I watched her interact with people. She seemed always to have time for others, to be genuinely interested in them, and to treat *everyone* with great dignity and respect. As I watched her it seemed that she literally "lifted" people and that they left her presence feeling better about themselves.

When I decided to pursue a doctorate degree I knew I wanted to study with Dr. Holbrook. I determined that the same books would be available at any university I attended, but that there were things I could learn from Leona Holbrook that couldn't be learned anywhere else or from anyone else. When I first told her of my interest in enrolling at Brigham Young University, she suggested I visit the campus before making a final decision. She knew of my smoking habit and that I dearly loved wine. Dr. Holbrook simply said, "BYU is a very unique place. Visit before you make your decision." More than a year before I became a student, I visited BYU. After a two-day visit I wrote, "My stop at BYU only served to convince me that I made the right decision. Having been there made me realize I'll even be able to give up my wine for what I'll receive in return."

Less than a month after my arrival in Provo, one of the women with whom I was living suggested I attend the groundbreaking service for the Provo Temple with her. I did not know the significance of that event, but what I saw and felt touched me deeply. I listened intently as a father quietly and patiently responded to the incessant questioning of his young family. He was kind and gentle as he held the children and talked with them. And then the people covering the hillside began singing "The Spirit of God Like a Fire Is Burning." They knew all the words without a hymnbook, and I felt the Spirit of God.

The following August, at the conclusion of summer school, I was given a leatherbound triple combination by a class of students who inscribed this message: "Dear Miss Rasmus, you have shared with us things that are important and close to you. In return, we would like to give you something that means a great deal to us. And we want you to know that we give it to you with a lot of love and respect. Sincerely, your fans, BYU Summer School, Second Session, 1970." It was to become the gift that made a difference. Though I could not begin to comprehend what it was they had really shared with me, I was touched that a group of students cared enough to present me with such a special gift. I tried reading the book, but it made little sense to me. Finally, instead of reading from the beginning, I read portions I'd heard others talk about or that I'd been told I should read. I remember reading Alma 32 and Moroni 10, but did not feel particularly impressed.

During the break between summer school and the beginning of fall semester, I drove to visit my family in Ohio, stopping to spend time with friends at Iowa State University. They were filled with questions about what Mormons were really like and what they did for fun. I felt I handled their inquiries with accuracy and good humor, but I was unprepared for a question asked me by one friend later that evening. "I've heard a lot about Joseph Smith," she began. "Was he really a prophet? Did he receive gold plates from an angel? Where did the Book of Mormon come from? Is it true?"

The questions sounded simple enough, but I didn't know the answers. In fact, I had never really given much thought to these things. It was a long drive from Iowa back to Utah. I had a lot of time to think and question and wonder. Are these things true? How can I really know? Again, I tried reading the Book of Mormon, but I understood little. The names and circumstances were unfamiliar to me. I'd heard people say this book was "for our time," but it didn't seem like that to me. It certainly didn't "speak to me."

Why had my friend asked me these questions anyway?

How did I know if Joseph Smith was a prophet? I had a copy of the Book of Mormon, and I'd read parts of it, but I didn't know if it was true or not. I tried to forget about these things, but they were constantly on my mind. I never talked with anyone about these things, but like Mary, "pondered them in [my] heart." (Luke 2:19.) I believe now I was afraid to explore these thoughts with anyone—afraid on the one hand that they might be true, and afraid on the other that they might not be.

About a month after the beginning of the fall semester, several of my friends invited me to accompany them on an all-day hike one beautiful Saturday in October. I was eager to leave my studies and head for the mountains. But, as it neared 10:00 A.M. they began looking for a comfortable place to sit down. I didn't have any idea it was General Conference weekend; in fact, I didn't even know what General Conference was. I certainly didn't know my friends were equipped with a transistor radio. I was, without question, a captive audience, and although I said nothing to any of the hiking group, when I returned home that evening I wrote on my daily calendar, "Everything sounds so right."

Shortly after that experience I decided to fast for the first time in my life. It was a day when I was also studying for a statistics test. I was unsettled and unable to concentrate on studying for the test. Finally, I knelt down to pray. I have no recollection of the prayer I offered, but these thoughts came into my mind and I felt impressed to record them on a scrap of paper: "October 12, 1970, 8:45 A.M. Go now, my child, for there is much work to be done. I send my Spirit to be with you to enable you to work and think clearly, to accomplish all that lies before you this day. Go now and know that I am with you in all things, and later return to me, coming to me with real intent of prayer. Know that I am the Lord, that all things are possible to them who call upon my name. Take comfort in these words. Fill your heart with joy and gladness, not sorrow and despair. Lo, I am with you always, even unto the end of the world. Know me as Comforter and Savior."

That evening I wanted to be alone. I went to my student office on campus, locked the door, turned out the lights, and prayed. I wanted answers to the questions I'd been asking. I didn't expect an angel to appear, but I wanted some kind of manifestation that would prove, once and for all, that these things were true or false.

Nothing happened! The experience earlier in the day had no particular meaning because I did not yet understand what Enos taught, that the voice of the Lord can come into our mind. (See Enos 1:10.) I also knew nothing about the principle of learning "by *study* and also by *faith*." (D&C 88:118.) Now I recognize I was like Oliver Cowdery in that I "supposed that [God] would give it unto [me], when I took no thought save it was to ask." (D&C 9:7.)

I left my office determined to forget about Joseph Smith, the Book of Mormon, and everything associated with The Church of Jesus Christ of Latter-day Saints. But I couldn't. These things seemed to be constantly on my mind. Several months later I had the impression that I should begin to pay tithing. For more than three months, each time I received a paycheck I took 10 percent of my meager student teacher wage and put the cash in a white envelope carefully hidden in a dresser drawer. I never had a desire to touch the money or to use it for something else. Although I wasn't sure how to give it to him, I believed it belonged to the Lord. I did other things that seemed and felt right. I would attend the Lutheran Church in the morning and then go with friends to sacrament meeting and Sunday School. I stopped drinking coffee, which had always seemed harmless to me and which I had never understood was part of the honor code I had promised to keep when I enrolled at BYU. I spent many hours helping a friend memorize the missionary discussions before she left for her mission.

I believe I felt impressed to do these things because "the Spirit giveth light to every man that cometh into the world; and the Spirit enlighteneth every man through the world, that hearkeneth to the voice of the Spirit." (D&C 84:46.) Elder Bruce R. McConkie explains, "It is this spirit that leads men to accept the gospel and join the Church so that they may receive the gift of the Holy Ghost." (*Mormon Doctrine* [Salt Lake City: Bookcraft, 1966], page 447.)

Only two weeks before I would join the Church, I sat in a sacrament meeting and the following words came pounding into my head: "Know that Joseph Smith was a prophet and that through him my Church has been restored in these latter days. Know that the Book of Mormon is the word of God. Know that my Church has been reestablished upon the earth in these latter days. Know that I intend for you to be baptized. Know, believe, do."

These thoughts went through my head day and night for a week. The next Sunday during the sacrament service as I passed the bread to my neighbor, another thought came into my mind: "How much longer can you pass by the bread of life?" Six days later, on March 6, 1971, I was baptized and became a member of The Church of Jesus Christ of Latter-day Saints.

Within a week of my baptism, I received a letter dated March 6 from a friend who was serving a mission in Brazil. She wrote: "It's 11:20 here in São Paulo, 7:20 there in Provo. I should be in bed, but for some reason I have a deep desire to visit with you. You have been in my thoughts, especially today. My thoughts won't let me rest in peace until I write." After telling me of her missionary work, she bore her testimony and concluded, "The unyielding need to communicate with you has been satisfied, and I am ready to go to bed. I go in peace knowing this is a special day, and we have shared together for a few moments."

Shortly I learned that my letter to her, mailed within an hour following my baptism, arrived in São Paulo on the day I received her letter. She wrote telling me that when she received my letter she told her companion before opening it, "This will be the letter telling me that my friend has joined the Church."

My experience with these letters taught me an important principle — the Spirit has power to communicate things in ways we do not understand. As is so often the case in our daily lives, events and circumstances that seem so ordinary and commonplace at the time of their happening take on deeper meaning in retrospect.

Throughout my life much of my interest in things of a spiritual nature has come about because of what I have observed in lives of others. I knew by the way in which my parents lived their lives that they not only *knew about* the first and second commandments, but they were committed to living them. My initial interest in the Mormon Church came as a result of what I observed in the lives of others — how people interacted with each other and how they treated me. A woman I remembered meeting only once left a homemade pie and a note on my doorstep. She wanted to welcome my mother who was coming to visit. At the time I knew nothing about visiting teachers or that she was mine. But I remember well my feelings that she had done this for me, that she knew who I was, and that she cared enough about me to take the time to do something special. Only after my baptism would I know that the Kockerhans family *always* made it a point to sit near me at every sacrament meeting. "Because," said the father of the family and the priesthood bearer who baptized me, "we wanted you to feel our spirit and our love for you." And, oh, how I did!

Many people and experiences formed a mosaic of beliefs that led to my decision to join The Church of Jesus Christ of Latter-day Saints. The process of learning about the gospel is one of the most exciting things I have ever done. I know that things are revealed to us when we "ask with a sincere heart, with real intent, having faith in Christ." (Moroni 10:7.)

I believe that the Book of Mormon is everything the Prophet Joseph Smith told us it was — "The most correct of any book on earth, and the keystone of our religion," and that we can "get nearer to God by abiding its precepts, than by any other book." (*History of The Church of Jesus Christ of Latter-day Saints,* 7 vols., 2d rev. ed., edited by B. H. Roberts [Salt Lake City: The Church of Jesus Christ of Latter-day Saints, 1932–51], 4:461.)

I have often referred to the Book of Mormon given me by a class of students as "the gift that made a difference." More accurately, it is the book that makes *all* the difference in each of our lives. Alma knew that "the preaching of the word had a great tendency to lead the people to do that which was just." He recorded that the word "had had more powerful effect upon the minds of the people than the sword, or anything else." No wonder Alma wanted the people to "try the virtue of the word of God." (Alma 31:5.) John said it another way, "If any man will do his will, he shall know of the doctrine." (John 7:17.)

I have "experiment[ed] upon [his] words." (Alma 32:27.) I have found them to be true, and they have made all the difference in my life. When I am discouraged or feeling depressed; when I am searching for answers or need to feel a power greater than my own; when I am in need of comfort or patience or increased faith — I turn to the scriptures and "try the virtue of the word of God." And I have never been disappointed.

Sometimes I feel, like Mormon, that "I cannot write the hundredth part" of what I know or have experienced or feel. (Words of Mormon 1:5.) With Nephi I desire to "talk of Christ, [to] rejoice in Christ, [and to] preach of Christ." (2 Nephi 25:26.) With Jacob I want others to know that I "knew of Christ" and that I have a "hope of his glory." (Jacob 4:4.) I want to do the things required by the Lord: to put my "trust in that Spirit which leadeth to do good—yea, to do justly, to walk humbly, [and] to judge righteously." (D&C 11:12.)

With all my heart I believe the invitation Moroni extended to each of us: "Come unto Christ, and be perfected in him, and deny yourselves of all ungodliness . . . and love God with all your might, mind and strength, then is his grace sufficient for you, that by his grace ye may be perfect in Christ." (Moroni 10:32.)

My desire in writing this book is that it will lead others to find and experience for themselves the "virtue of the word of God." Contained in the pages of holy writ are insights, answers, knowledge, and wisdom—all that we need to win every battle and conquer every foe. What is promised in the scriptures is true: In the strength of the Lord we can do all things.

PART I
THE CHALLENGE

Chapter One

Signs of the Times

Charles Dickens began his famous book *A Tale of Two Cities* with the oft-quoted line, "It was the best of times. It was the worst of times." Although he was describing the French Revolution, his statement seems to also apply to the times in which we live.

In many ways we do live in the best of times. As a matter of routine we enjoy such conveniences as dishwashers, clothes dryers, electric blankets, air conditioners and automobiles. We enjoy fast foods, frozen foods, and low-fat foods. This is the age of rapid transportation. Today we can fly in comfort and luxury to countries our grandparents only read about. Computers make the storing, cataloging, and retrieval of information easy and instantaneous. Improved health conditions and medications have eliminated many life-threatening diseases. Open heart surgery, hip and knee replacements, cornea transplants, and other surgeries not only extend life but enhance the quality of life. Through the medium of modern-day electronics we have immediate access to events occurring anywhere in the world by simply turning a dial on a radio or television set. Although many still talk of the "good old days," few want to surrender the time-saving modern-day conveniences that eliminate physical labor, protect our health, and enhance our life-style. Certainly, in some respects, we are living in the "best of times."

But with new inventions and life-style changes come new challenges. How do we learn the importance of taking care of things when many products are disposable and designed to be thrown away, rather than cared for and preserved? How do we learn to "bridle all [our] passions" (Alma 38:12) when shopping center marquees flash messages telling us to indulge our "passion with fashion"? How do we learn to be "submissive, meek, [and] humble" (Mosiah 3:19) when billboards tell us to "super boost our ego"? How do we put off the "natural man" when faced with a steady stream of advertising suggesting that "thin and rich" is both wonderful and essential; that "right" labels are important; and that success is measured by the size of one's financial holdings and material possessions?

Though often perceived as a miracle, television can also be a menace. This modern-day invention brings into our homes programs which openly flaunt immoral behavior and suggest that instant gratification is not only pleasurable, but acceptable. Through all forms of media we are made aware of serious social ills—increasing teenage pregnancy, drug and substance abuse, violent crimes, divorce, suicide, abortion, AIDS, and lack of ethics. Such social symptoms suggest that perhaps these are indeed the "worst of times."

Living in Perilous Times

But we should not be surprised. We are living in the last days, days which the Apostle Paul described as "perilous."

These are times in which "men shall be lovers of their own selves, covetous, boasters, proud, blasphemers, disobedient to parents, unthankful, unholy, without natural affection, trucebreakers, false accusers, incontinent, fierce, despisers of those that are good, traitors, heady, highminded, lovers of pleasures more than lovers of God." (2 Timothy 3:1–4.)

Nephi also described a time which sounds much like our own. He says there shall "be many which shall say: Eat, drink, and be merry; nevertheless, fear God—he will justify in committing a little sin; yea, lie a little, take the advantage of one because of his words, dig a pit for thy neighbor; there is no harm in this." (2 Nephi 28:8.)

A modern-day prophet, President Ezra Taft Benson, has told us that "our generation will be comparable in wickedness to the days of Noah, when the Lord cleansed the earth by flood." However, he indicates that there will be a major difference this time. "God has saved for the final inning some of his strongest and most valiant children who will help bear off the kingdom triumphantly." That, he tells us, is where we come in. For we are "the generation that must be prepared to meet [our] God." He acknowledges that "never before on the face of this earth have the forces of evil and the forces of good been so well organized" but reminds us that the outcome has already been determined— "the forces of righteousness will finally win." He then continues, "What will remain to be seen is where each of us now and in the future will stand in this battle—and *how tall* we will stand." Great battles can make great heroes and heroines.

In addition to the "societal battles" between good and evil and right and wrong, President Benson tells us that "each of us has his or her own battlefield." (Ezra Taft Benson, "In His Steps," devotional address given in Anaheim, California, 8 February 1987.)

Regardless of age, marital status, educational background, or economic circumstance, everyone faces personal but very differing challenges on a daily basis. Young married couples often struggle to have enough money to meet basic needs as they begin a new family unit. Older people are sometimes challenged by ill health during their retirement years. Single adults often feel lonely and unwanted. There are others who stoop under the burden of physical or emotional pain or a handicap of some kind. Parents of teenagers are faced with challenges ranging from keeping up with everyone's schedule to responding to an adolescent's serious questioning about such issues as peer pressure, the role of men and women in today's society and in the Church, abortion, premarital sex, and ethics.

Single parents carry heavy burdens without having another adult to share the load. Parents whose children are raised sometimes feel lonely or abandoned, and don't know how to cope with the "empty nest years." Others may find themselves serving as parents to their grandchildren. Young adults face critical issues and decisions revolving around dating, missions, marriage, family, careers. Those in middle age are challenged to balance demands of work with quality family life and service to neighbors, church, and community.

Amid such challenges or "battles," many people talk of feeling stressed, anxious, depressed, frustrated, overly committed, and overwhelmed. When offered alternatives that promise immediate pleasure, freedom from pain, and instant gratification, increasing numbers of youth and adults are turning to drugs or seeking to gratify their natural desires by winning social acceptance or purchasing worldly possessions. When things aren't going very well, we fail to recognize that trials are meant to be blessings—evidences of our Heavenly Father's love for us. "Whom the Lord loveth he chasteneth." (Hebrews 12:6.) Trials and temptations provide opportunities for growth.

Though in many ways we live in the best of times, there are battles raging—in society, in the world, and often within our families and in our personal lives. Though not fought with swords or cimeters or guns, the battles in which we are engaged are just as real and as potentially deadly. The Book of Mormon, compiled to be read by us in our day, contains many accounts of battles fought by the people of that time. Although the enemies they fought were very different than those we face today, the methodology they used can be instructive for us.

Go Forth in the Strength of the Lord

Repeatedly, the Book of Mormon contains the phrase "in the strength of the Lord." We read of King Benjamin and his armies fighting against the Lamanites. *"In the strength of the Lord* they did contend against their enemies, until they had slain many thousands of the Lamanites." (Words of Mormon 1:14.) Zeniff records, "I and my people did go forth against the Lamanites to battle. Yea, *in the strength of the Lord* did we go forth . . . ; for I and my people did cry mightily to the Lord that he would deliver us out of the hands of our enemies." Zeniff then bears testimony saying, "God did hear our cries and did hear our prayers; and *we did go forth in his might."* (Mosiah 9:16–18.)

On another occasion Zeniff again speaks of battling against the Lamanites. "And it came to pass that we did go up *in the strength of the Lord* to battle." (Mosiah 10:10.) He continues, "I did stimulate them to go to battle with their might, *putting their trust in the Lord."* (Mosiah 10:19.) Likewise, in an epistle to Moroni, Pahoran talks of taking possession of the city of Zarahemla: "We will go forth against them *in the strength of the Lord,* and we will put an end to this great iniquity." (Alma 6:18.) In the same letter he tells Moroni to "strengthen Lehi and Teancum in the Lord; tell them to fear not, for *God will deliver them.*" (Alma 6:21.)

Others in the Book of Mormon refer to being able to go forth and to conquer "in the strength of the Lord." As Moroni went among the people waving the Title of Liberty, he cried with a loud voice, saying, "Behold, whosoever will maintain this title upon the land, let them come forth *in the strength of the Lord.*" (Alma 46:20.) Likewise, the newly converted King Lamoni acknowledged to Ammon, "I know, *in the strength of the Lord thou canst do all things.*" (Alma 20:4.) Ammon, wanting not to boast of his own strength or wisdom, acknowledged that "as to my strength I am weak; therefore I will not boast of myself, but I will boast of my God, for *in his strength I can do all things.*" (Alma 26:12.)

Although the battles of our day are of a very different nature, these lessons from the Book of Mormon suggest that victory over our enemies (whoever or whatever they may be) is assured if we go forth "in the strength of the Lord."

How do we do this? How do we call upon "the strength of the Lord" as we cope with the increasing challenges and complexities of life? How do we find the peace promised in the scriptures amid hectic and busy times? How do we develop the kind of faith that enabled people of other times to work miracles and to trust so completely in the Lord? How do we gain access to the kind of power that caused people to move forward with optimism in the face of difficulty and often seemingly impossible challenges?

How do we come to experience and believe that "the words of Christ . . . will tell [us] all things what [we] should do?" (2 Nephi 32:3.) Alma taught that "the preaching of the word had a great tendency to lead the people to do that which was just," and that it had a "more powerful effect upon the minds of the people than the sword or anything else." Because of this, Alma believed that the Zoramites should "try the virtue of the word of God" (Alma 31:5), or in other words, try living the word of God in their daily lives that they might experience its power. If the "word" can have such a powerful effect in our lives, how do we become familiar with his words so that we might "try" them and learn of their "virtue" or worth? Indeed, how do we liken the scriptures to our lives and apply their messages to help us with our battles?

In an age when many are distrustful, skeptical, and afraid, we can read of Christ's invitation to all to "look unto me in every thought; doubt not, fear not." (D&C 6:36.) How do we come to believe in and accept this invitation to eliminate doubt and fear from our lives?

In the book of Alma we are told to "cry unto God for all [our] support" and to "counsel with the Lord in all [our] doings, and he will direct [us] for good." (Alma 37:36–37.) Do we have the faith to believe that this promise is for us? Are we willing to humble ourselves and cry unto God for *all* our support? Do we truly believe *he will* direct us for good? Perhaps like the apostles of old we say, "Lord, increase our faith." (Luke 17:5.) But how does this happen? How do we strengthen our faith, especially in a time when so many demand evidence or seek for a sign?

The purpose of this book is to explore ways in which we might better understand "the strength of the Lord" and the power that is available to us as we face our own challenges and the "battles" of our day. President Benson tells us we will "never have a better opportunity to be valiant in a more crucial cause than in the battles [we] face today and in the immediate future." (Ezra Taft Benson, "In His Steps.")

This book is intended as a personal testimony and witness that there is a very real power available to each of us through Jesus Christ. With faith in him, we will be victorious as we "go forth in the strength of the Lord."

PART II

THE WAY

Chapter Two

By His Grace
We Have Power

Perhaps one of the most important lessons each of us needs to learn is that we are not alone on this earth, and that the "plan" is not for us to fail but for us to succeed and ultimately to return to our heavenly parents. The purpose for our earthly existence is to give us experience. (See D&C 122:7.) That experience is sometimes joyful and happy. At other times we experience frustration and discouragement. But in every situation, at every age, and whatever our experience, we have the promise of Jesus Christ, "Lo, I am with you alway, even unto the end of the world." (Matthew 28:20.)

We need not face each day, each challenge, each opportunity for growth alone. We can go forth "in the strength of the Lord." But how do we do this?

There is a higher power accessible to each of us every day, every hour. It is the same power by which worlds were made. It is the power of faith. The Bible Dictionary defines *faith* as "a principle of action and of power, and by it one can command the elements and/or heal the sick, or *influence any number of circumstances when the occasion warrants*." (LDS Edition of the King James Version, The Church of Jesus Christ of Latter-day Saints, 1983, "Bible Dictionary," page 669.) The Book of Mormon prophet Jacob, writing of the people of his day, said, "Our faith becometh unshaken, insomuch that we truly can command in the name of Jesus and the very trees obey us, or the mountains, or the waves of the sea." (Jacob 4:6.)

Then he taught a great lesson, explaining *why* they "have power to do these things." He said, "The Lord God showeth us our weakness that we may know it is by his grace, and his great condescensions unto the children of men, that we have power to do these things." (Jacob 4:7.)

Like many of us, Jacob and his people might have doubted their abilities or wondered how they could accomplish the challenges placed before them. When we feel overwhelmed, unsure of ourselves, or unable to cope, we are in essence acknowledging our "weaknesses" — the difficulties we have in doing those things that need to be done. Yet, as Jacob explains, we are given "weakness" by our Heavenly Father so that "we may know that it is by his grace . . . that we have *power*." (Jacob 4:7.)

A Divine Means of Help or Strength

What exactly is this "grace" that is given us? The Bible Dictionary tells us "the main idea of the word *grace* is a divine means of help or strength, given through the bounteous mercy and love of Jesus Christ." (LDS Edition of the King James Version, "Bible Dictionary," page 697.) Grace is an "enabling power." Through Christ's love and mercy, we can have access to "a divine means of help or strength" — literally, an "enabling power."

Many scriptures contain the word *grace*. If we substitute

the words *enabling power* for the word *grace*, scriptures take on a new meaning. Consider the following:

"Let us therefore come boldly unto the throne of grace, that we may obtain mercy, and find [an enabling power] to help in time of need." (Hebrews 4:16.)

In the second epistle of Paul to the Apostle Timothy, he counsels him to "be strong in the [enabling power] that is in Christ Jesus." (2 Timothy 2:1.)

Ether records the words of the Lord which tell us "my [enabling power] is sufficient for the meek," and that "if men come unto me I will show unto them their weakness. I give unto men weakness that they may be humble; and my [enabling power] is sufficient for all men that humble themselves before me; for if they humble themselves before me, and have faith in me, then will I make weak things become strong unto them." (Ether 12:26–27.)

These scriptures suggest that part of the reason we feel "weak" is so we will acknowledge that we do indeed need a strength beyond our own. Our weaknesses turn us to Jesus Christ. It is through our faith in him and his mercy and love for us that we come to know that there is a "divine means of help or strength available to each of us." The Apostle Paul must have understood this well, for he wrote in his letter to the Philippians, "I can do all things through Christ which strengtheneth me." (Philippians 4:13.)

Likewise, many composers of hymns written in this dispensation acknowledge our dependence upon Christ for strength beyond our own:

> *"I need thee, oh, I need thee;*
> *Every hour I need thee!*
> *Oh, bless me now, my Savior;*
> *I come to thee!*
> > ("I Need Thee Every Hour," Hymns of
> > The Church of Jesus Christ of Latter-
> > day Saints, 1985, no. 98.)

25

"I will not doubt, I will not fear;
God's love and strength are always near.
His promised gift helps me to find
An inner strength and peace of mind.
I give the Father willingly
My trust, my prayers, humility.
His Spirit guides; his love assures
That fear departs when faith endures.
("When Faith Endures," Hymns, no. 128.)

Faith — A Principle of Action and of Power

There *is* a power available to us. This power is faith—
a principle of action and of power. It is through the bounteous mercy and love of Jesus Christ that we receive his
grace—a divine means of help or strength.

The principles of faith and grace can literally empower
us to "go forth in the strength of the Lord." The power
available to us through Jesus Christ is very real. But while
we have access to it, we are required to do our part.

If you have flown on an airplane, you know that prior to
takeoff the flight attendant makes an announcement similar
to the following: "Your oxygen mask is located in the com-
partment above your seat. If needed, it will drop down automatically. If you are smoking and see the masks, please
extinguish your cigarette. Pull the mask towards you firmly
to start the oxygen flowing. Place the mask over your nose
and mouth and slip the elastic band over your head. For
those traveling with someone who will need assistance, put
on your mask first and then assist them with an additional
mask."

Consider the implications of this announcement. Everyone has an oxygen mask located above their seat. If necessary, it will drop down automatically. However, nothing
will happen unless the passenger pulls the mask toward him
to firmly start the oxygen flowing.

Oxygen is needed to sustain mortal life. Without it, we will die. Likewise, we need the enabling power of the Savior to help us sustain our spiritual lives. Jesus Christ has said to us, "I am come that they might have life, and that they might have it more abundantly." (John 10:10.) On another occasion after Christ had fed the five thousand, he told those gathered that he was "the bread of life." (John 6:48.) Numerous times Christ referred to himself as the "light and the life of the world." (See Mosiah 16:9; Alma 38:9; 3 Nephi 9:18; Ether 4:12; D&C 11:28; D&C 12:9; D&C 45:7.)

The oxygen mask hanging above our heads does us no good unless we pull it firmly toward us and place the mask over our nose and mouth. Likewise, Christ's power is inoperable in our lives until *we* humble ourselves, acknowledge our dependence upon him, and invite him into our life. "Behold, I stand at the door, and knock: if any man hear my voice, and open the door, I will come into him, and sup with him, and he with me." (Revelation 3:20.)

Two other aspects of this pre-takeoff announcement provide parallels related to gospel principles. Passengers are told that if they are smoking and see the masks, they are to extinguish their cigarettes. Perhaps we should "extinguish from our lives" anything that would interfere with our fully receiving the gift of life. Should we not eliminate from our lives those practices and sins and wrongdoings which would prevent us from receiving Christ into our lives?

The announcement also tells us that we are first to put on our own mask before we assist small children traveling with us. In other words, we must first receive the oxygen and be strong in order that we might help others. So it is in the matter of faith. Before we can strengthen the faith of others, we must first be strong in faith. Christ tells Simon Peter, "I have prayed for thee, that thy faith fail not." He then adds, "When thou art converted, strengthen thy brethren." (Luke 22:32.)

The announcement given on the airplane tells us that we have access to life-giving oxygen. To have access to this life-giving substance, *we* must activate it. The scriptures tell us that we have access to a life-giving power through Jesus Christ. To activate this power we must believe in Jesus Christ and have faith in him and in his power. Such belief will not only change our lives, but enable us to live life to its fullest.

Chapter Three

Faith Comes by Hearing

H ow do we strengthen or develop our faith in the Lord Jesus Christ? Paul told the Romans that "faith cometh by hearing." (Romans 10:17.) The Bible Dictionary tells us that "faith is kindled by hearing the testimony of those who have faith. Miracles do not produce faith, but strong faith is developed by obedience to the gospel of Jesus Christ; in other words, faith comes by righteousness, although miracles often confirm one's faith." (LDS Edition of the King James Version, "Bible Dictionary," page 669.)

As we seek to increase our faith, it is helpful to listen to the testimony of those who have witnessed God's power in their lives and who testify of the reality of miracles.

A friend of mine, who was raised on a ranch in Arizona, told me of an experience she had as a child. Her father had promised that a foal about to be born would be hers. The day the foal was born she was in the barn and got to witness the event. She watched in wonder and amazement. Suddenly the mare rolled over on the foal, crushing its tiny body. As soon as the mother horse moved a bit, my friend jumped into the stall and cradled the lifeless foal in her arms. With all the faith of a child, she cried out to Heavenly Father to save her horse. Shortly, the little animal began to breathe and the long thin legs began to tremble.

Unbeknownst to my friend, her father had observed the last part of this drama. At that point he entered the stall and, embracing his daughter, said words to this effect, "When you live the best you know how to live, and when you pray to Heavenly Father, he can work miracles."

Several years ago, against the advice of some friends, I purchased a used motorbike. It was old and small and at top speed went only forty miles per hour. Believing I was in no danger traveling at such a slow speed, I *chose* not to wear a helmet. I loved to feel the wind in my hair. One Saturday afternoon I filled the tank with gas and started up a slightly inclined street. The next thing I remember was hearing a man say, "Don't move. We've called the paramedics." I was aware of a strange feeling on the left side of my face. When I lifted my hand there I discovered that the left side of my face was bloodied and broken.

Among the crowd of people which gathered was a friend who had recognized my bike and stopped. She took my hand in hers. I said simply, "Bonnie, I need a priesthood blessing."

Almost immediately I was strapped to a stretcher and taken by ambulance to the hospital. Almost as quickly, two men who held the Melchizedek Priesthood were at my side. I remember only one phrase of the blessing: "Thou shalt be fully restored and more."

During the following days, weeks and months, each time I moved my head I heard a strange gurgling noise. In a near panic I pictured my brains moving from one side of my head to the other. Then *always* the phrase from that priesthood blessing came to my mind, "Thou shalt be fully restored and more," and I was calmed. After months of slow and painful healing, I was fully restored and more.

Would I have recovered without the priesthood blessing, or was there a connection between the blessing promised and my eventual healing? I feel certain that that blessing, coupled with my prayers and the prayers of many friends, made *all* the difference.

An Age of Great Skepticism

Bruce C. Hafen, former president of Ricks College and currently the provost of Brigham Young University, wrote about a university student who had a childhood experience similar to that of my Arizona friend. After relating the incident to his priesthood quorum, this student said, "I tell you that story because I don't think I would do now what I did then. Now that I am older, less naive, and more experienced, I 'know better' than to expect help in that kind of situation. I am not sure I would believe now, even if I relived that experience, that [it] was anything more than a coincidence. I don't understand what has happened to me since that time, but I sense that something has gone wrong."

Brother Hafen added, "Whatever the change in attitude was, I too sensed that it was not healthy. Did it matter? He still came to church, but he had become less childlike, less believing. His sense of the miraculous had waned. Yes, it should have been a matter of great concern." ("Is Yours a Believing Heart," *Ensign*, September 1974, pages 52–57.)

We live in a day and an age of great skepticism. People demand "proof." There is a feeling among many that unless something can be measured and analyzed, it does not exist or at the very least is of little value.

Like Korihor the anti-Christ in the Book of Mormon, many suggest and even insist that "ye cannot know of things which ye do not see." (Alma 30:15.) Korihor believed that the holy prophets desired to keep the people in "bondage." He accused the priests of yoking the people "by their traditions and their dreams and their whims and their visions and their pretended mysteries." (Alma 30:28.) Korihor wanted evidence. He challenged Alma by demanding, "Show me a sign." (Alma 30:43.)

There are many Korihors in the world today, many who demand evidence and seek for a sign. Often genuine spiritual experiences are referred to as coincidence. It is suggested that "some things just happen."

Alma's response to Korihor is instructive. He says, "Thou hast had signs enough; will ye tempt your God? Will ye say, Show unto me a sign, when ye have the testimony of all these thy brethren, and also all the holy prophets? The scriptures are laid before thee, yea, and all things denote there is a God; yea even the earth, and all things that are on the face of it, yea, and its motion, yea, and also all the planets which move in their regular form do witness that there is a Supreme Creator." (Alma 30:44.)

Perhaps a coincidence could be defined as "a small miracle in which God chooses to remain anonymous." (As quoted by Patricia T. Holland, "One Thing Needful: Becoming Women of Greater Faith in Christ," *Ensign*, October 1987, pages 26–33.)

Hope for Things Which Are Not Seen, Which Are True

Often, as is the case with most spiritual things, we struggle to put into words what we feel and believe and know. A number of years ago, Ardeth G. Kapp, Young Women General President, was asked to speak to a group of young women one early morning in the high Uintah mountains. At the conclusion of her remarks she asked each young woman to find a quiet spot in nature and, before returning home, to "talk with your Father in Heaven and share with him the things that are in your heart." She told them that "he is always there and he will hear you."

Two weeks later during a testimony meeting in Sister Kapp's own ward, Becky, the assistant youth camp director, stood to add her testimony to those of the other girls who had participated in this same camping experience: "Something about the feelings I had that special morning made me want to be alone for a while, so I found a private spot where there was a little opening in the trees. When I knelt down on the ground, thick with pine needles, I didn't know for sure what to say, so I closed my eyes and said, 'Heavenly Father, do you know I am here?' I waited and waited and I could hear the wind in the trees. Then I opened my eyes and saw the sun coming through the leaves, and I felt all warm inside." She paused a moment and then, in a reverent whisper, added, "You may not think it was anything, but I know he knew I was there." (Ardeth G. Kapp, *Miracles in Pinafores and Bluejeans* [Salt Lake City: Deseret Book Co., 1979], pages 39–40.)

Do we know that Heavenly Father knows that we are here? Do we "hope for things which are not seen, which are true"? (Hebrews 11:1; Alma 32:21.) Do we have faith to "influence any number of circumstances when occasion warrants"? (LDS Edition of the King James Version, "Bible Dictionary," page 670.) Do we really believe that through the mercy and love of Jesus Christ we have access to a divine means of help or strength if we will but humble ourselves, acknowledge our weaknesses, and call upon him? That is our challenge, our responsibility—to figuratively pull the oxygen mask down, as was described in an earlier chapter, and begin to breathe deeply of the spiritual life-giving substance that comes from the Savior of the world.

33

Faith Comes by Hearing the Word of God

The scriptures teach us about faith and give evidences of the power of faith. This is one of the reasons that Alma believed the scriptures have a "powerful effect" upon people. (Alma 30:5.) He knew what Paul wrote and the Prophet Joseph Smith later taught, that "faith comes by hearing the word of God." (*Teachings of the Prophet Joseph Smith* [Salt Lake City: Deseret Book Co., 1976], page 148.)

Nephi tells us that the reason he labored diligently to write was to "persuade our children, and also our brethren, to believe in Christ, and to be reconciled to God." He continued: "It is by grace that we are saved, after all we can do. . . . We are made alive in Christ because of our faith. . . . [We] may look forward unto that life which is in Christ."

He concludes, "The words which I have spoken shall stand as a testimony . . . for they are sufficient to teach any man the right way; for the right way is to believe in Christ." (2 Nephi 25:23, 25, 27–28.)

The prophet Ether cried from morning "even until the going down of the sun." He wanted the people to know the power of faith — "that by faith all things are fulfilled." Like many in our day, the people "did not believe, because they saw [great and marvelous things] not." (Ether 12:3, 5.)

Moroni adds to Ether's record by saying, "Dispute not because you see not, for ye receive no witness until after the trial of your faith." (Ether 12:6.)

Moroni then recounts the wonders and marvels accomplished through the power of faith. (See Ether 12.) He cites the following evidences of faith (see also Paul's testimony of the power of faith in Hebrews 11): It was by faith that Christ appeared to the faithful (Ether 12:7); by faith the Law of Moses was given and by faith the "more excellent way" prepared by Christ has been fulfilled (Ether 12:11); the faith of Alma and Amulek caused the prison to tumble to the earth (Ether 12: 13); the faith of Nephi and Lehi wrought a change upon the Lamanites who were then baptized with fire and the Holy Ghost (Ether 12:14); the faith of three disciples resulted in their obtaining a promise that they would not taste death (Ether 12:17); and the faith of the brother of Jared was so great that when God put forth his finger he could not hide it from him (Ether 12:20).

After listing these examples of great faith, Moroni taught an important principle: "If there be no faith among the children of men God can do no miracle among them." (Ether 12:12.) Mormon taught the same thing when he testified, "The reason why [God] ceaseth to do miracles among the children of men is because that they dwindle in unbelief." (Mormon 9:20.) This same principle is described in the writings of Matthew: "And [Jesus] did not many mighty works there because of their unbelief." (Matthew 13:58.) Likewise, we have the words of Mormon recorded by his son Moroni, "For it is by faith that miracles are wrought . . . wherefore, if these things have ceased wo be unto the children of men, for it is because of unbelief." (Moroni 7:37.)

From our study, several things are evident: first, faith *is* "a principle of action and of power"; second, true faith must be centered in Jesus Christ; third, the scriptures give evidence of the power of faith in the lives of people; fourth, where there is *no* faith, miracles cannot occur.

How do we increase our faith? What are the things we can do in our lives to work miracles for the Lord? How do we increase our faith in Jesus Christ so that we can lay aside fear, worry, and other things that prevent us from being all that we can be and doing all that we can do?

Chapter Four

Increase Our Faith

C hrist taught his disciples "hard doctrine" when he said: "No servant can serve two masters: for either he will hate the one, and love the other; or else he will hold to the one, and despise the other. Ye cannot serve God and mammon." (Luke 16:13.) He told the story of a certain rich man and of a beggar named Lazarus. While in this life the beggar sought to be fed by the rich man. After death it was the rich man who cried out that Lazarus, the beggar, might "dip the tip of his finger in water, and cool my tongue." (Luke 16:24.) Next, Christ taught the disciples that if their brother were to trespass against them seven times in a day that they should still forgive him. (Luke 17:4.)

No doubt some of the Savior's followers, wanting to believe, struggled with how they might follow his teachings. There were times when, after hearing Christ's teachings, some of them would reply, "This is an hard saying," and at times some even turned and "walked no more with him." (John 6:60, 66.)

However, Luke records that following Christ's teachings "the apostles said unto the Lord, increase our faith." (Luke 17:5.)

Like the apostles, we often desire to believe but struggle because our faith is weak. We too cry, "Lord, increase our faith."

Many of us can relate to the father who brought his son to Christ to be healed. It appears that the son might have experienced what we know today as epilepsy, for the father told Christ that he "fell on the ground" and that he "foameth, and gnasheth with his teeth." The father says that often his disease had "cast him into the fire, and into the waters, to destroy him." (Mark 9:18, 20, 22.)

The father then says to Christ, "If thou canst do any thing, have compassion on us, and help us." (Mark 9:22.)

Christ's instructions to the father are equally applicable to us. He replied, "If thou canst believe, all things are possible to him that believeth." (Mark 9:23.)

The father's response is so much like ours when we go to Christ knowing that he can help and that we need his help so badly. The scriptures say that the father "said with tears, Lord, I believe; help thou mine unbelief." (Mark 9:24.) Subsequently, the child was healed.

There are many who do believe but who, like the apostles and followers of Christ anciently, desire to increase their faith. How do we strengthen our belief and increase our faith?

As I read and study, observe others who I believe are of a strong faith, and seek to increase my own faith, several things emerge as being helpful in strengthening faith.

Before suggesting three principles which can strengthen our faith, let me give a caution. There is no such thing as a "magic formula" which, when followed, eliminates problems, stresses, and hard times. Even Christ, in his agony in the Garden of Gethsemane, prayed unto the father that, if it was possible, "let this cup pass from me." He then added an important qualifying phrase: "Nevertheless not my will, but thine, be done." (Luke 22:42; see also Matthew 26:39; Mark 14:36.) In this case the cup was not, and could not be, removed. Nevertheless, the Father came to the aid of his Only Begotten Son: "And there appeared an angel unto him from heaven, strengthening him." (Luke 22:43.)

Having been *strengthened*, Jesus Christ went forth to accomplish his foreordained mission—the ultimate sacrifice, the great Atonement.

While miracles do happen, and we may well, through the appropriate exercise of faith, have some obstacles removed from our paths, there are many things which will not be "removed from us"; however, with faith in Jesus Christ and through his bounteous mercy and love, we can experience his grace—a divine means of help and strength and power sufficient to deal with the challenges life presents us.

It is helpful to review the Prophet Joseph Smith's experience while a prisoner at the Liberty Jail in Missouri in 1839. He cried to the Lord, imploring him to stretch forth his hand and stop the "wrongs and unlawful oppressions" directed at the suffering saints. He pleaded with the Lord to "remember thy suffering saints." (See D&C 121:3, 4, 6.)

The wrongs and oppressions did not cease (as often ours will not), but the Lord poured out an even greater blessing, the blessing of peace, and then he explained to the Prophet: "Thine adversity and thine afflictions shall be but a small moment; And then, if thou endure it well, God shall exalt thee on high; thou shalt triumph over all thy foes." (D&C 121:7–8.)

During his life, President Spencer W. Kimball, twelfth president of The Church of Jesus Christ of Latter-day Saints, suffered typhoid fever, smallpox, Bell's palsy, years of boils and carbuncles, a major heart attack, cancer of the throat which resulted in the removal of most of his vocal cords, reoccurrence of cancer which required radiation treatment, and heart disease that led to open heart surgery to replace a valve and transplant an artery. Yet he continued to give unselfish service in building the kingdom of God. He exemplified one who learned how to "walk by faith." (2 Corinthians 5:7.) He wrote:

> Just as undaunted faith has stopped the mouth of lions, made ineffective fiery flames, opened dry corridors through rivers and seas, protected against deluge and drought, and brought heavenly manifestations at the instance of prophets, so in each of our lives faith can heal the sick, bring comfort to those who mourn, strengthen resolve against temptation, relieve from the bondage of harmful habits, lend the strength to repent and change our lives, and lead to a sure knowledge of the divinity of Jesus Christ. Indomitable faith can help us live the commandments with a willing heart and thereby bring blessings unnumbered, with peace, perfection, and exaltation in the kingdom of God. (Spencer W. Kimball, *Faith Precedes the Miracle* [Salt Lake City: Deseret Book, 1972], page 12.)

And so it can be as we "increase our faith." Challenges, temptations, hardships, and difficulties will not always be removed from us; but by the power of faith in the Savior we can feel peace, experience comfort, and realize a strength and power which comes only through belief in him.

Three principles which I believe can literally increase our faith are: first, searching the scriptures; second, being in tune with the Spirit of the Lord; and third, praying always.

I am not suggesting that these are the only things which increase our faith, but I have a personal testimony that these are true principles that enhance and contribute to our ability to go forth "in the strength of the Lord."

The chapters that follow contain personal insights I have gained as I have sought to understand faith and to strengthen my own faith. I share them as seeds of thought which I hope you will plant and nourish, eventually participating in a personal harvest of faith.

In writing about faith, I am not suggesting that I have perfect faith. There are many times when my faith wanes or when I wish I could be more firm in my faith. I take consolation from President Kimball's comment that "we would not have much motivation to righteousness if all speakers and writers postponed discussing and warning until they themselves were perfected." (Spencer W. Kimball, *The Miracle of Forgiveness* [Salt Lake City: Bookcraft, 1969], page xii.)

Chapter Five

Search the Scriptures

Alma taught the multitudes of people who gathered upon the hill Onidah about faith and the word of God. He explained that faith is not a perfect knowledge (see Alma 32:21, 26) and suggested that the same was true of the word of God which he preached unto them: "Ye cannot know of their surety at first . . . any more than faith is a perfect knowledge." (Alma 32:26.)

Then Alma taught a powerful lesson, a lesson that applies both to the development of faith and to the understanding of the word of God. He said: "If ye will awake and arouse your faculties, even to an experiment upon my words, and exercise a particle of faith, yea, even if ye can no more than desire to believe, let this desire work in you, even until ye believe in a manner that ye can give place for a portion of my words." (Alma 32:27.)

Awake, arouse, experiment, exercise, desire — these are action words. They require action on our part. Repeatedly throughout the scriptures we are directed to take action —

to ask, believe, receive, desire, inquire, knock, ponder, nourish, and so forth.

In describing the devil, Nephi tells us that the Adversary will pacify and lull the people into carnal security (see 2 Nephi 28:21). No wonder we are told to be awake and alert.

In comparing "the word" to a seed, Alma tells us that if it is a good seed, "or that the word is good," it will begin to enlarge our soul. It will begin to enlighten our understanding and be delicious to us. (Alma 32:28.) Then he adds, "Would not this increase your faith?" (Alma 32:29.) Alma implies that it is through the word that our faith can increase.

In modern times Elder Bruce R. McConkie taught something similar: "Faith is . . . born of scriptural study. Those who study, ponder, and pray about the scriptures, seeking to understand their deep and hidden meanings, receive from time to time great outpourings of light and knowledge from the Holy Spirit." Elder McConkie suggested that "faith comes and revelations are received as a direct result of scriptural study." Notice Elder McConkie's use of action words—*study, ponder, pray, seek.* (See "Holy Writ: Published Anew," Regional Representative's Seminar, 2 April 1982.)

A Desire to Believe

If our study of the scriptures can increase our faith, how do we begin? Again, the scriptures are instructive. Alma has told us that it is sufficient if we can "no more than desire" to believe. (Alma 32:27.)

Lehi, the first prophet in the Book of Mormon, received a vision of the tree of life. His son, Nephi, "having heard all the words of [his] father, concerning the things which he saw in a vision" (1 Nephi 10:17), wanted to know of the vision for himself. "I, Nephi, was desirous also that I might see, and hear, and know of these things, by the power of the Holy Ghost, which is the gift of God unto all those who diligently seek him." (1 Nephi 10:17.)

The account of Nephi preparing for and receiving the vision of the tree of life is filled with action words: "For it came to pass that after I had *desired* to know the things that my father had seen, and *believing* that the Lord was able to make them known unto me, as I sat *pondering* in my heart I was caught away in the Spirit of the Lord." (1 Nephi 11:1.) Nephi's experience is the same as Alma's counsel. First he desired, then he believed.

This is reinforced in Nephi's experience. After he had been "caught away . . . into an exceedingly high mountain," the Spirit said to him, "Behold, what desirest thou?" (1 Nephi 11:2.) Nephi *knew* what he desired. He said, "I desire to behold the things which my father saw." (1 Nephi 11:3.) Then the Spirit said to him, "Believest thou that thy father saw the tree of which he hath spoken?" Nephi responded, "Yea, thou knowest that I believe all the words of my father." (1 Nephi 11:4–5.) Then the Spirit said to Nephi, "Blessed art thou, Nephi, because thou believest in the Son of the most high God; wherefore, thou shalt behold the things which thou desirest." (1 Nephi 11:6.)

The beginning of our scripture study must start with our desire to believe. (Alma 32:27.) When Alma tells us that we must "give place for a portion of my words," could he mean that we must find a place (or a time) in our fast-paced, often hectic lives to study and ponder the scriptures?

Active Participation

In the analogy of the oxygen mask on the airplane (see chapter two), oxygen becomes available only when action is taken by the passengers — when they pull the line and mask toward them. So it is with the study of the scriptures.

To understand the scriptures requires that we be active participants.

Nephi's experience in receiving the vision gives us another clue that can be helpful to us in our own study of the scriptures. We know that he had a desire to know about the vision and that he believed the Lord could make it known unto him. But we also read that prior to the vision Nephi "sat pondering." To ponder means "to consider something deeply and thoroughly; to weigh carefully in the mind; to consider thoughtfully." A synonym for *ponder* is *meditate*. (*The Random House Dictionary of the English Language,* unabridged, 1966.) We have many scriptures which illustrate the things that happened as people pondered or meditated.

The revelation recorded in D&C 76 provides one such example. The Prophet Joseph Smith had been commanded by the Lord to translate the Bible, and he indicated that "it was apparent that many important points touching the salvation of man had been taken from the Bible, or lost before it was compiled." (Joseph Smith, *History of The Church,* 1:245.) In the process of doing this work, Joseph and Sidney Rigdon came to John 5:29, which differed in the translation from the King James Version. The Prophet recorded, "Now this caused us to marvel, for it was given unto us of the Spirit. And while we meditated upon these things, the Lord touched the eyes of our understandings and they were opened, and the glory of the Lord shown round about." (D&C 76:18–19.) Joseph and Sidney were actively involved — they meditated. It was then that a great vision was shown them: They saw the Father and the Son and recorded one of the most powerful testimonies in all the holy scriptures: "And now, after the many testimonies which have been given of him, this is the testimony, last of all, which we give of him: That he lives! For we saw him, even on the right hand of God; and we heard the voice bearing record that he is the Only Begotten of the Father—That by him, and through him, and of him, the worlds are and were created, and the inhabitants thereof are begotten sons and daughters unto God." (D&C 76:22–24.)

We have record of a similar experience preceding a vision given to Joseph F. Smith, the sixth president of the Church, recorded in D&C 138. He reported: "On the third of October in the year nineteen hundred and eighteen, I sat in my room pondering over the scriptures; And reflecting upon the great atoning sacrifice that was made by the Son of God, for the redemption of the world; . . . While I was thus engaged, my mind reverted to the writings of the apostle Peter. . . . I opened the Bible and read the third and fourth chapters of the first epistle of Peter. . . . As I pondered over these things which are written, the eyes of my understanding were opened and the Spirit of the Lord rested upon me." (D&C 138:1, 2, 5–6, 11.)

What follows is President Smith's description concerning the Savior's visit to the spirit world. Note the action words recorded in this section: *pondering, reflecting, opened,* and *pondered.*

Nephi, the son of Helaman, had a similar experience. He was pondering over the things which the Lord had shown unto him. "And it came to pass as he was thus pondering . . . in his heart" that the voice of the Lord came unto him. He was commended for his "unwearyingness," was given the sealing power, and was commanded to declare the word of the Lord unto the people. (Helaman 10:2–4, 12.)

When Jesus Christ showed himself unto the people of Nephi and preached unto the multitudes, he, too, instructed the people to ponder. He perceived that they did not understand all of the words he had spoken to them and he said, "Go ye unto your homes, and ponder upon the things which I have said, and ask of the Father, in my name, that ye may understand, and prepare your minds for the morrow." (3 Nephi 17:3.) *Ponder, ask, prepare* — all are action words.

Interestingly, we have no direction in the scriptures themselves to merely read the scriptures. We are always told to search or study or ponder. Probably each of us have had the experience of reading passages of scripture, only to finish and realize that we're not even sure we know what we've read. Learning requires an investment of time and energy. We must be mentally awake and actively involved in the learning process.

King Benjamin learned this lesson from an angel, who appeared unto him and said, "Awake, and hear the words which I shall tell thee; for behold, I am come to declare unto you the glad tidings of great joy." (Mosiah 3:2–3.) The scriptures contain glad tidings of great joy, but we must be awake to understand their messages.

In the analogy of comparing the word to a seed, Alma repeatedly admonishes the people to "nourish it." (See Alma 32:37–42.) He tells the people that they cannot have "fruit" unless they nourish the word. How is it to be nourished? He repeats three words three times — by *diligence, faith*, and *patience.* (See Alma 32:41–43.) To nourish is to cherish, foster, and keep alive. Diligence is constant, persistent, and earnest effort. Patience is quiet perseverance. Faith is to hope for things which are true. (See Alma 32:21.)

In summary, searching the scriptures requires action on our part. We begin simply by having a desire to learn. That desire must be nourished with faith and diligence and patience.

Becoming Acquainted with the Scriptures

During his tenure as President of the Church, President President Spencer W. Kimball delivered several landmark addresses to the women of the Church. In 1978 he counseled the sisters to "study the scriptures that you may gain strength through understanding of eternal things. You . . . need this close relationship with the mind and will of our Eternal Father. We want our sisters to be scholars of the scriptures as well as our men. You need an acquaintanceship with his eternal truths." ("Privileges and Responsibilities of Sisters," *Ensign*, November 1978, page 102.)

The following year, in 1979, he again emphasized the importance of scriptural study: "I stress again the deep need each woman has to study the scriptures. We want our homes to be blessed with sister scriptorians — whether you are single or married, young or old, widowed or living in a family. Become scholars of the scriptures — not to put others down, but to lift them up!" ("The Role of Righteous Women," *Ensign*, November 1979, page 102.)

President Ezra Taft Benson has repeatedly admonished members of the Church to study the scriptures. He has told us to "immerse [our]selves in the scriptures regularly and consistently." ("Cleansing the Inner Vessel," *Ensign*, May 1986, pages 4–7.) Further, he has said that we will be denied the sweet whisperings of the Spirit unless we "pay the price of studying, pondering, and praying about the scriptures" ("The Power of the Word," *Ensign*, May 1986, pages 79, 82), and that we must come to see that "studying and searching the scriptures is not a burden laid upon [us] by the Lord, but a marvelous blessing and opportunity" ("A Sacred Responsibility," *Ensign*, May 1986, pages 77–78). President Benson has promised that "if we will daily sup from [the Book of Mormon] and abide by its precepts, God will pour out upon each child of Zion and the Church a blessing hitherto unknown." ("The Savior's Visit to America," *Ensign*, May 1987, pages 4–7.)

My initial serious desire to read the scriptures came as a result of President Kimball's admonition to become scholars of the scriptures. As I listened to our prophet, I knew it was the right thing to do. In the past I had read verses and chapters and sometimes pages, understanding little of what I read and remembering very little. I was aware of frequently repeated scriptures and I knew where to find things such as the Beatitudes or Christ's discourse on the first and second great commandments. But I was reading strictly out of obedience, because I thought I should.

At that stage of life my reading of the scriptures could be likened to having to practice musical scales or arpeggios. My piano teacher said that these drills would make me a better pianist. I couldn't see how. I didn't like doing it, but I responded in obedience. Later, as my skill in piano increased, I found that many patterns in music came easier because I was familiar with the fingering from previous drills. My constant drilling of scales and arpeggios nourished my understanding of and skill in playing the piano. I practiced with faith (I believed what my piano teacher told me), with diligence (my mother made sure my effort was constant and persistent), and patience (perseverance).

Just as practice made me more comfortable with piano music, I found that constant repetition of studying the scriptures helped me become more comfortable with the language of the scriptures. I would mark the scriptures when I heard others make reference to them in a sacrament meeting or conference talk. In addition to marking them, I would usually write the date in the margin and sometimes who had made reference to it. I would do the same thing if I read an article which gave me new insight into a scripture. Often I would jot a note in the margin to help me better understand the meaning of the scripture.

As I became more acquainted with the scriptures, I began

to see patterns emerge. I remember my excitement one morning as I read Mosiah 3:19. In talking about yielding to the enticings of the Holy Spirit and becoming a Saint through the atonement of Christ, King Mosiah uses these words: "submissive, meek, humble, patient, full of love." I remembered reading some of these same words in the New Testament. Using the Topical Guide I was soon able to turn to the fifth chapter of Galatians: "But the fruit of the Spirit is love, joy, peace, longsuffering, gentleness, goodness, faith, meekness, temperance." (Galatians 5:22–23.) The footnote lead me to Colossians 3:12 in which similar words were used to describe the elect of God. I turned again to the Topical Guide to look up each of the words I originally read in Mosiah and was lead to such scriptures as Helaman 3:35, Alma 7:23–24, D&C 4:5–6, and D&C 121:41–42. I was having my own scripture chase and loving it!

Like seeing portions of scales and arpeggios repeated in music, I became increasingly aware of repeated words (*faith, diligence,* and *patience*) and ideas. Although the references identified in the new LDS editions of the scriptures lead us to the Topical Guide or Bible Dictionary or other scriptures, I found myself adding to the information that was available when I found another scripture that seemed to me equally related.

Likening the Scriptures unto Ourselves

But the real key to searching the scriptures and enjoying them came when I followed Nephi's advice to liken the scriptures unto ourselves. (See 1 Nephi 19:23–24.) One day as a friend and I were sharing favorite scriptures, she told me one of the ways in which she "likened the scriptures" to herself. Each time she was reading and felt that a scripture "applied" directly to her, she wrote in the margin "to me" and put the date under it. I began doing this. I remember one period of time when I was feeling particularly discouraged. I was trying to do things that seemed right, but I felt as though I was taking one step forward and two steps backward, and making little overall progress. In the midst of this period of discouragement, I read from Alma 7:19: "For I perceive that ye are in the paths of righteousness; I perceive that ye are in the path which leads to the kingdom of God; yea, I perceive that ye are making his paths straight." I felt as though the Lord was speaking directly to me, that he acknowledged that I was trying to live my life in an appropriate way. As I read the scripture, I wept and felt that the message was just for me. I wrote in the margin "to me," and underneath put the date.

Over a period of about three years I have identified thirty-six such scriptures. In addition to writing in the margin of the scriptures, I also have kept a list on the very last page. Recently, I began at the top of the list and reviewed each scripture one after the other. I was surprised to realize that more than half of the scriptures dealt with the need for having patience. I was struck with the significance of that message to me and felt that the scriptures were, as Nephi tells us, "for our profit and learning." (1 Nephi 19:23.)

On a trip to Ohio to visit my parents who are in their mid-eighties and dealing with the challenges of aging, my mother said to me, "I feel just like Job." I sensed her discouragement and despair, and thought about what I might say to her that would be comforting and helpful. Almost immediately the words of the Prophet Joseph Smith recorded in D&C 121 came into my mind. He had pleaded with the Lord and asked some hard questions concerning the suffering of the saints in Missouri. He wanted the Lord to kindle his anger against their enemies and to "avenge us of our wrongs." (D&C 121:5.) Then came the voice of the Lord to the Prophet Joseph (and I believe to my mother): "Peace be unto thy soul; thine adversity and thine afflictions shall be but a small moment; And then, if thou endure it well, God shall exalt thee on high. . . . Thy friends do stand by thee. . . . Thou art not yet as Job; thy friends do not contend against thee, neither charge thee with transgression, as they did Job." (D&C 121:7–10.)

I could hardly wait to share this scripture with my mother. Early the next morning I told her about the Prophet Joseph Smith and the many adversities the Saints had suffered in Missouri. I then read her this portion of scripture. Together we talked about Job and all that he had endured. We also talked about the many blessings and good things for which she had to rejoice. When we finished talking she said simply, "I am not at all like Job. I have so many things for which to be thankful."

As my mother and I talked that morning I gained new insights from her and we were led to read the scriptures about Job. I have found that sharing and discussing scriptures with others is a wonderful way to expand my own knowledge and to learn from others. Sometimes I'll call a friend on the phone and say, "Listen to this" or, "I got a new insight this morning while I was reading the scriptures. Do you have a minute for me to share?" Other friends of mine have found that reading and discussing the scriptures together is an exciting process. A group of women I know walk early every morning; they walk and talk and learn together. Known affectionately in the neighborhood as the "traveling synagogue," they use as their "course of study" the standard works. What a wonderful way to become physically and spiritually fit!

Ye Do Err, Not Knowing the Scriptures

The scriptures help us understand the importance of searching and knowing the scriptures. Because Nephi desired to know the things that his father had seen, he was shown the vision of the tree of life. (See 1 Nephi 11.) However, Nephi's brothers did not understand the teachings of their father and "were disputing one with another concerning the things which [their] father had spoken unto them." They said to Nephi, "We cannot understand the words which our father hath spoken." (1 Nephi 15:2, 7.) Nephi himself admits that the things spoken by Lehi were "hard to be understood, save a man should inquire of the Lord." He asked his brothers, "Have ye inquired of the Lord?" (1 Nephi 15:3, 8.) The Lord then counseled, "If ye will not harden your hearts, and ask me in faith, believing that ye shall receive, with diligence in keeping my commandments, surely these things shall be made known unto you." (1 Nephi 15:11.)

In at least three instances scripturally, people are rebuked for not having searched and known the scriptures. In the New Testament the Sadducees asked Christ a question concerning the writings of Moses. They wanted to know if a man married his brother's widow, whose wife would she be in the Resurrection. Jesus answered, "Ye do err, not knowing the scriptures, nor the power of God." (Matthew 22:29; Mark 12:24.)

In the Book of Mormon we have record of the Zoramites believing that they could not worship God because they were not permitted to enter into the synagogues. (See Alma 32:3.) Alma said to them, "Behold, ye have said that ye could not worship your God because ye are cast out of your synagogues. But behold, I say unto you, if ye suppose that ye cannot worship God, ye do greatly err, and ye ought to search the scriptures; if ye suppose that they have taught you this, ye do not understand them." (Alma 33:2.) Moroni spoke to the unbelievers who did not believe in revelations, prophecies, gifts, healings, or the speaking with and interpretation of tongues. He said, "He that denieth these things knoweth not the gospel of Christ; yea, he has not read the scriptures; if so, he does not understand them." (Mormon 9:7–8.)

Not knowing the power of God or understanding his ways is only one consequence of not searching the scriptures. In scriptures referring to the last days we read that the time will come when "they that murmured shall learn doctrine." (See Isaiah 29:24; 2 Nephi 27:35.) Elder Neal A. Maxwell suggests that this could be interpreted to mean that "doctrinal illiteracy is a significant cause of murmuring among church members." ("A Choice Seer," *Ensign*, August 1986, page 9.)

It is instructive to look at scriptures containing the words *murmur* and *murmured*. A few illustrations demonstrate that when the people were not acquainted with the ways of the Lord, they murmured:

"And all the children of Israel murmured against Moses and against Aaron: and the whole congregation said unto them, Would God that we had died in the land of Egypt! or would God we had died in this wilderness!" (Numbers 14:2.) If the children of Israel had understood what Moses knew about their exodus to the promised land, they would not have murmured.

"And the Pharisees and scribes murmured, saying, This man receiveth sinners, and eateth with them." (Luke 15:2.) The pharisees and scribes did not understand that Christ came to save sinners, therefore they murmured.

"The Jews then murmured at him, because he said, I am the bread which came down from heaven." (John 6:41.) Although the Jews could understand that manna had been sent from heaven to save ancient Israel from starvation and temporal death, they did not understand that the bread which Christ would give was his flesh. (See John 6:51.) Not only did the Jews murmur because they did not understand this doctrine, but we are told many of the Savior's disciples believed that this was "an hard saying" and many "walked no more with him." (John 6:60, 66.)

"Because of the stiffneckedness of Laman and Lemuel . . . they did murmur in many things against their father, because he was a visionary man, and had led them out of the land of Jerusalem." (1 Nephi 2:11.)

If Laman and Lemuel had truly understood that being a "visionary man" meant that their father walked and talked with God, they would not have murmured. Also, they would have known that to remain in Jerusalem would have meant that they might have been destroyed.

"And thus Laman and Lemuel . . . did murmur against their father." In this instance the scriptures tell us why they murmured — "because they knew not the dealings of that God who had created them." (1 Nephi 2:12.)

Is it possible that we sometimes murmur because we are not familiar with or do not understand or have not taken the time to study and learn the doctrine?

The Scriptures Enlarge Our Memory

When Alma entrusted the records to his son Helaman, he also commanded him to keep a record of the people, "for it is for a wise purpose that they are kept." (Alma 37:2.) He indicates that all the records which have been preserved were done so in the wisdom of God. Alma tells his son that one of the reasons these records have been preserved is that they might enlarge the memory of the people. (See Alma 37:8.) Our memory is those impressions or recollections or remembrances of the past. In this scripture Alma tells us that one of the purposes of the scriptures is to help us remember. The word *remember* (and its variants — *remembered, rememberest, remembereth,* and *remembering*) appear 461 times in the Standard Works, 193 of which are in the Book of Mormon alone. Although the people were told to remember a variety of things, five themes recur in these "remember" scriptures: One, *remember* to keep his commandments and to observe the statutes of the Lord (see 1 Nephi 15:25; 2 Nephi 1:16; Mosiah 1:7; Alma 9:13; Alma 37:13, 35); two, *remember* God's mercy toward us (see Alma 29:10; Alma 32:22; Moroni 10:3); three, *remember* the great things God has done for us and for his people (see Alma 9:9; Alma 29:11, 12; Mosiah 27:16); four, *remember* Christ's atoning sacrifice and means of salvation (see 1 Nephi 19:18; Helaman 5:9, 12); and five, *remember* the teachings of those who taught of God (see Helaman 4:21; Helaman 5:10; Alma 33:3; Alma 46:24; Alma 57:21; Ether 15:1).

As we study the scriptures we can learn about God, his dealings with men throughout the ages, the gift of Jesus Christ to each of us, and the testimony of others who believed in God. As we study these things, our memories will be enlarged and we will increase our understanding of things pertaining unto God.

The Scriptures Testify of Jesus Christ

Amulek taught the people, repeating what his "beloved brother" Alma had said unto them; that they needed to "prepare [their] minds" and have faith to "plant the word in [their] hearts" so that they could "try the experiment of [the word's] goodness." (Alma 34:1–4.)

The most important reason for us to search the scriptures is to increase our faith in Jesus Christ, for the scriptures teach and write and testify of Christ. Jacob records that "none of the prophets have written, nor prophesied, save they have spoken concerning this Christ." (Jacob 7:11.) He also indicated that "for this intent have we written these things, that they may know that we knew of Christ, and we had a hope of his glory many hundred years before his coming." (Jacob 4:4.)

Nephi recorded that the things he wrote were to persuade his people that they would remember the Lord their Redeemer (see 1 Nephi 19:18). He also wrote, "We labor diligently to write, to persuade our children, and also our brethren, to believe in Christ, and to be reconciled to God." (2 Nephi 25:23.) Writing to us in our day, Mormon says, "For this cause I write unto you . . . that ye may believe the gospel of Jesus Christ." (Mormon 3:20–21.) Alma instructed his son, Helaman, that the records "should be kept and handed down from one generation to another, and be kept and preserved by the hand of the Lord to bring them to the knowledge of the Lord their God, and to rejoice in Jesus Christ their Redeemer." (Alma 37:4, 9.)

It is for this reason that the scriptures are laid before us — that we might know of Jesus Christ, have faith in him, partake of his goodness and power, and be blessed with his grace which will enable us to "go forth in the strength of the Lord."

Chapter Six

Having His Spirit to Be with Us

Faith in the Lord Jesus Christ cannot be known or developed "but [by] the Spirit of God." (1 Corinthians 2:11.) It is through "the spirit which is of God that we might know the things that are freely given us of God." (1 Corinthians 2:12.) Paul also tells us that there are things which we cannot learn through "the words which man's wisdom teacheth" but which must be learned through the Holy Ghost. (1 Corinthians 2:13.)

The Prophet Joseph Smith understood this same principle when he said, "It requires the Spirit of God to know the things of God." (*Teachings of the Prophet Joseph Smith,* page 205.) The prophet Jacob bore testimony that the works of the Lord are "great and marvelous . . . [and] unsearchable are the depths of the mysteries of him." He wrote, "It is impossible that man should find out all his ways. And no man knoweth of his ways save it be revealed unto him." (Jacob 4:8.)

Following a vision given to the Prophet Joseph Smith

and Sidney Rigdon in 1832, they bore witness in much the same way that Jacob did. "Great and marvelous are the works of the Lord, and the mysteries of his kingdom . . . which surpass all understanding in glory, and in might, and in dominion." (D&C 76:114.) They too tell us that such things are "only to be seen and understood by the power of the Holy Spirit." (D&C 76:116.) Job also taught this principle for he said to his three friends, "The inspiration of the Almighty giveth . . . understanding." (Job 32:8.)

Since each of us is a literal child of God, our spirits having been born to Heavenly Parents before we came to earth to receive bodies from our mortal parents, it is not surprising that God would continue to give understanding to our spirits. (See Hebrews 12:9.) There is great truth to the statement by Teilhard de Chardin: "We are not human beings having a spiritual experience. We are spiritual beings having a human experience." It is through God's spirit that he communicates to us, his children. Therefore, being in tune with his spirit is critical to our learning and remembering and knowing the things of God.

Repeatedly, the prophets of this dispensation have admonished us to be in tune with the Spirit of the Lord. The Prophet Joseph Smith said, "I know that His spirit will bear testimony to all who seek diligently after knowledge from Him." (*Teachings of the Prophet Joseph Smith*, page 29.) Following the death of the Prophet Joseph Smith he appeared in February of 1847 to President Brigham Young. President Young asked the Prophet Joseph if he had a message for the people. The Prophet said, "Tell the people to be humble and faithful, and be sure to keep the Spirit of the Lord and it will lead them aright. Be careful and not turn away from the still small voice; it will teach you what to do and where to go; it will yield the fruits of the kingdom." (*Manuscript History of Brigham Young*, February 23, 1847.)

Similarly, President Wilford Woodruff was visited by President Brigham Young about two years after President Young's death. President Woodruff asked Brigham Young if he had a message for the Saints in Arizona. President Young said, "Tell the people to get the Spirit of the Lord and keep it with them." (As quoted by Neal A. Maxwell, *Not Withstanding My Weaknesses* [Salt Lake City: Deseret Book, 1981], page 113.)

In our day President Ezra Taft Benson has said, "Spirituality—being in tune with the Spirit of the Lord—is the greatest need we all have. We should strive for the constant companionship of the Holy Ghost all of our days. Seek the Spirit in all you do. Keep it with you continually." ("Seek the Spirit of the Lord," *Ensign*, April 1988, page 5.)

The Spirit Will Enlighten Our Minds

How does the Spirit work on and with us? How do we recognize it? The scriptures give us insight. The Lord, through a revelation given to Joseph Smith, said, "I will impart unto you of my Spirit, which shall enlighten your mind." (D&C 11:13.) In teaching how to recognize the promptings of the Spirit, the Prophet Joseph Smith explained that sometimes we "feel pure intelligence" flowing into us, or we receive "sudden strokes of ideas." These things, presented to our minds, come by the Spirit of God. "Thus by learning the Spirit of God and understanding it, [we] may grow into the principle of revelation" (*Teachings of the Prophet Joseph Smith*, page 151.)

In a revelation given through Joseph Smith to Oliver Cowdery, the Lord said, "I will tell you in your mind and in your heart, by the Holy Ghost, which shall come upon you and which shall dwell in your heart. Now, behold, this is the spirit of revelation." (D&C 8:2–3.)

Enos prayed mightily and gained a remission of his sins. He continued to cry unto the Lord "in mighty prayer and supplication" all day long and through the night. Then he received a revelation: "There came a voice unto me, saying: Enos, thy sins are forgiven thee, and thou shalt be blessed." (Enos 1:4–5.)

I, like you, have had experiences when, at critical times, important thoughts have come into my heart and mind.

I remember one such morning when I finished my prayers and stood almost before I'd uttered, "Amen." I was ready to grab my coat and leave for work when the thought came into my mind, "Go back and kneel beside your bed." Even though I felt pressed for time, the impression came so strongly that I responded immediately.

As I returned to my knees a scripture came into my mind: "I will go before your face. I will be on your right hand and on your left . . . and mine angels round about you, to bear you up." (D&C 84:88.) That was all. I stayed there for a few minutes, all the time wondering why that scripture would come into my mind. Then I left for work.

It is about a forty-five minute drive from my home in Orem, Utah, to my work in Salt Lake City. I knew that a storm had been forecasted, but the sun shone brightly as I left home and I went merrily on my way. About twenty minutes later, as I neared what is referred to locally as the point of the mountain, I drove into a blinding snowstorm. The snow was heavy enough that I struggled even to see the white line marking the edge of the freeway; to keep my bearings I had to focus on the tail lights of the eighteen-wheeler ahead of me. Suddenly, and without warning, the truck swerved into the median strip of the highway.

The storm was bad enough that the radio station I was

listening to kept advising people to stay off the highways. One caller indicated that this was the worst weather conditions he'd seen in the Salt Lake Valley in twenty-five years. I concurred, as I was driving at a snail's pace. The snow was turning to ice as it hit the highway, and the visibility continued to decrease.

What cars were still on the road were sliding across the various lanes; and many cars were off to the side of the road. Though I gripped the steering wheel tighter and tighter, I felt that I had little or no control of the car. It almost seemed inevitable that I'd be the next car off the highway or involved in an accident.

Suddenly the experience I'd had less than an hour earlier came into my mind. As the words of the scripture passed through my mind again, I felt an immediate sense of peace and calm. I *knew* that I would be safe, that I would be protected on my right and on my left.

It took three times longer than usual to get to work that morning, but I did get there. I was safe, and once again I knew that the influence of the Spirit in our lives is real, and that it can serve as both a guide and a comfort.

The Spirit Speaks Peace to the Mind

One of the most common ways that we feel the influence of the Spirit is described in D&C 6:23. The Lord says to the Prophet Joseph, "Did I not speak peace to your mind concerning the matter? What greater witness can you have than from God?"

Late one night when I felt particularly harried and rushed, I knelt to pray. I was so tired I don't remember saying much more than, "Heavenly Father, please help me." Shortly thereafter, I felt impressed to reach for a pad of paper and pencil. While still on my knees, I wrote these words which came to my mind:

When all around seems strange and wrong,
I seek to know what's right.
I pull away to be alone,
I seek to find the light.

The Spirit whispers, I feel at peace.
I know God cares and hears.
Eternal truth rings in my ears,
My soul no longer fears.

Oh, Heavenly Father, hear my prayer
And calm my troubled mind.
Help keep my thoughts in thee alone,
Eternal truths to find.

My responsibilities and pressures and hectic schedule didn't change, but I did feel *peace*. And I sensed I was not alone. I knew that with the help of the Savior, I could do all that was expected and required — and that I could do it cheerfully and with his spirit.

Actively Seeking for the Spirit

If, through the Spirit of the Lord, we can have our minds enlightened, experience pure intelligence, hear the voice and receive the thoughts of the Lord in our mind, and feel peace, what must we do to have his Spirit with us? When manifestations of the Spirit of the Lord are recorded in the scriptures, the person receiving the manifestation is almost always actively engaged in the process of seeking direction, answers to specific questions, or insight into a situation. Nephi, wanting to know the things concerning the vision his father had received, was "desirous . . . [to] see, and hear, and know of these things, by the power of the Holy Ghost, which is the gift of God unto all those who diligently seek him." (1 Nephi 10:17.)

Enos, before having the voice of the Lord come into his mind, tells us that his "soul hungered," he cried unto God "in mighty prayer and supplication," and he "poured out [his] whole soul unto God." (Enos 1:4, 9.)

The words which President Joseph F. Smith uses to describe his activity prior to having the Spirit of the Lord rest upon him are also words of action — *pondering, reflecting,* and *reading.* (See D&C 138:1, 2, 6.) The Prophet Joseph Smith received additional words of revelation concerning baptisms for the dead after this subject "occupied his mind" and "pressed itself upon [his] feelings." (D&C 128:1.)

Be Still and Listen

As in the study of the scriptures, we must be actively involved in the process of seeking — to know, to understand, or to receive an answer to our inquiry. Active listening is as critical as asking.

An incident from the life of Bishop John Wells, a former counselor in the Presiding Bishopric, teaches the importance of being guided by the Spirit.

Bishop Wells was a great detail man and was responsible for many Church reports. One of his sons was killed in a railroad accident on October 15, 1915. He was run over by a freight car. Sister Wells could not be consoled. She received no comfort during the funeral and continued her mourning after her son was laid to rest. Bishop Wells feared for her health, as she was in a state of deep anguish. One day, soon after the funeral, Sister Wells was lying on her bed in a state of mourning. The son appeared to her and said, "Mother, do not mourn, do not cry. I am all right." He then related to her how the accident had taken place. Apparently there had been some question — even suspicion — about the accident because the young man was an experienced railroad man. But he told his mother that it was clearly an accident. He also told her that as soon as he realized he was in another sphere, he had tried to reach his father but could not. His father was so busy with the details of his office and work that he could not respond to the promptings. Therefore, the son had come to his mother. He then said, "Tell Father that all is well with me, and I want you not to mourn any more." (Ezra Taft Benson, "Seek the Spirit of the Lord," *Ensign*, April 1988, page 2, as quoted in David O. McKay, *Gospel Ideals* [Salt Lake City: Improvement Era, 1953], pages 525–26.)

President Ezra Taft Benson has emphasized that "we must always be responsive to the whisperings of the Spirit. These promptings most often come when we are not under the pressure of appointments and when we are not caught up in the worries of day-to-day life." ("Seek the Spirit of the Lord," page 2.)

We live at a time when people seem always to be in a hurry, to be rushing from one appointment or place to another. There are appointments to keep, schedules to meet, and places to be; but in all of the rushing, where are we going?

We seem, somehow, to believe that to accomplish something we must be physically involved; that to have approval, either of ourselves or others, we must give an accounting of our activities during every waking hour. Somehow we believe that the more we do, the better we are.

At various times in my life when I've been caught up in the push-push, rush-rush way of living, my body has rebelled and I have finally had to justify to myself a reason to stop. The doctor would always confirm — "it was strep throat." I came to realize that although the manifestation was strep throat, it really was "stress throat."

During one of these illnesses, I lay in bed reflecting on a priesthood blessing I had received which included these words from Mosiah: "It is not requisite that a man should run faster than he has strength." (Mosiah 4:27.) Was I running faster than I had strength? I thought about and pondered this through the night. The next morning I reread Mosiah 4:27 and then D&C 10:4: "Do not run faster or labor more than you have strength and means." I began to think of many self-imposed deadlines. I thought of pushing beyond what I knew to be wise. In many cases it was because of false pride—I wanted to be seen as capable. I believed others' acceptance of me was dependent on the things I did.

Alone and not feeling physically like doing anything, I reflected not only on having run faster and labored harder than I had strength to do, but became aware that my prayers had been rushed. I could not remember having felt any prompting of the Spirit for some time, and my study of the scriptures was nonexistent. I made a quiet resolve to better "pace myself" and to be about the things that can, in fact, bring not only insight but also strength.

I recalled an experience I had had only weeks earlier. The kitchen floor seemed *always* to be dirty. I know two dogs and two people can track in a lot of dirt, but I was sweeping the floor every day, only to find that it looked just as bad the next day. I swept the kitchen floor every day for more than two weeks. Then one evening while repeating the exercise, I discovered that what really needed sweeping was the garage, through which entrance was gained to the kitchen. The next Saturday I cleaned the garage thoroughly. It was filthy, absolutely filled with dirt and dead grass and other debris. Immediately I found that the kitchen floor was much less dirty. While all that time I had been doing something right— I had done a fine job of sweeping the kitchen floor—I simply had not been doing the right or smart thing, which was keeping the garage clean. When the garage was clean, the kitchen floor remained cleaner.

Are our lives sometimes like that? Do we do things right, but not always do the right things? Do we sometimes rush around in a busy fashion, doing worthwhile things, but then never find time for the very things that bring peace and insight and strength from above? Do we sometimes not read the scriptures, or seek to listen to the Spirit, or pray and seek for answers because there's never quite enough "quiet" time for pondering, reading, and seeking?

The more I thought about this during that occasion of forced rest due to illness, the more it became evident that I needed to make some changes in my life. I went to my desk with several books and my scriptures and put together a memo that began: "To Carolyn Rasmus, from Carolyn Rasmus."

At the top I wrote two scriptures. "Do not run faster or labor more than you have strength and means" (D&C 10:4), and, "It is not requisite that a man should run faster than he has strength." (Mosiah 4:27.)

I added five quotes from the book *Notwithstanding My Weakness* (Deseret Book, 1981), by Neal A. Maxwell:

> Paced progress is essential; God used six measured and orderly creative periods followed by respite. (Page 5.)

> There is a difference between being steadily and effectively and "anxiously engaged" and being frantically engaged one moment and being passive the next. (Page 15.)

> Let us remember that the Lord *does not* want us to be weary by the way. (Page 15.)

> Steady devotion is better than periodic exhaustion. (Page 7.)

> Pace is so essential to personal progress lest we magnify our weaknesses instead of our callings. (Page 7.)

It seemed as though Elder Maxwell had written these statements just for me. I reviewed notes from a meeting I had attended during which Elder J. Thomas Fyans, a member of the First Quorum of the Seventy, had instructed the auxiliary leaders of the Church: "Do not create self-imposed deadlines that keep you out of breath."

Finally I turned to the scriptures to find what I knew was already there. In the New Testament there are numerous references to Christ going up into a mountain—sometimes to pray, sometimes to simply be alone. (See Matthew 5:1; 14:23; Mark 3:13; Luke 6:12; John 6:15.) One particular scripture was especially meaningful to me. The Apostles were with Jesus Christ, and they "shared with him what they had done and what they had taught." Following this "reporting session," Christ said to them, "Come ye yourselves apart into a desert place, and rest a while: for there were many coming and going, and they had no leisure so much as to eat. And they departed into a desert place by ship privately." (Mark 6:31–32.)

I noticed some parallels from these verses with my own life. Certainly there were "many coming and going" and "no leisure so much as to eat." I felt as if this scripture was just for me—"Come ye . . . and rest a while."

We see this same principle spoken of in the Book of Mormon. Alma had journeyed to the land of Gideon, taught the people, and "established the order of the Church." Then "he returned to his own house at Zarahemla to rest himself from the labors which he had performed." (Alma 8:1.)

In another instance, after Alma and Amulek had been imprisoned, contended with unbelievers, and taught the gospel, Alma took Amulek "to his own house, and did administer unto him in his tribulations, and strengthened him in the Lord." (Alma 15:18.)

If we are to be in tune with the Spirit, we must stop long enough to listen to its promptings. But listening can also be a challenge, especially when we are surrounded by family members, friends, telephones, radios, television sets, and compact disc players. This is especially challenging for those who live or work with teenagers. While serving as a ward advisor in the Young Women's program, I frequently drove young women who believed in a principle I called "ICRO" — "In Car . . . Radio On." And when the radio was on, it was loud. When the radio, or anything else for that matter, blares, all communication stops. Amid their protests that I was "the worst advisor they had ever had," I finally won out and we actually drove places *without* the radio on. At first they didn't know how to talk to each other, but gradually that changed. We not only learned about each other, but we learned to share, to communicate, and to listen to one another.

If we are to be in tune with the Spirit of the Lord we must "turn off" the noise of the world in order to listen, truly listen, to his voice. We need to remember that when the Lord spoke to Elijah it was *not* "a great strong wind [which] rent the mountains, and brake in pieces the rocks," it was not "in the earthquake" or "in the fire"; instead, the voice of the Lord came to Elijah as a "still, small voice." Likewise, when the voice of the Lord came to the people in the land of Nephi, "it was not a voice of thunder, neither was it a voice of a great tumultuous noise, but behold, it was a still voice of perfect mildness, as if it had been a whisper, and it did pierce even to the very soul." (Helaman 5:30.)

Numerous times in the scriptures we read words to this effect: "Be still and know that I am God." (See D&C 101:16; Exodus 14:13; Psalm 46:10.) However, it is in the Doctrine and Covenants that we learn why the Lord wants us, on occasion, to be still. He says to us, "Stop, and stand still until I command thee, and I will provide means whereby thou mayest accomplish the thing which I have commanded thee." (D&C 5:34.)

We dare not allow ourselves to become so caught up in the pressures of living that we remove ourselves from the true source of life. It is when we are still and quiet that we can hear the still, small voice helping us understand the deeper wisdom that comes from the Lord.

Unfortunately, we are sometimes our own worst enemy, imposing guilt on ourselves when we think we have not done as much as we could, or when we see others doing more. Elder Dallin H. Oaks suggested some general principles which, although specific to family history work, have a broader application. The first principle is that our efforts (in this case to promote temple and family history work) should be such as to accomplish the work of the Lord, not to impose guilt on his children. He then tells us that there is a variety of individual circumstances which must be taken into account if we are to eliminate imposing guilt. He specifically mentions "age, health, education, place of residence, family responsibilities and financial circumstances."

His second principle focuses on our need to understand that "in the work of redeeming the dead, there are many tasks to be performed." He suggests that we prayerfully select those ways that would fit our personal circumstances at a particular time. He says, "This should be done under the influence of the Spirit of the Lord." ("Family History: In Wisdom and Order," *Ensign*, June 1989, page 6.)

Prepare to Receive the Spirit

Perhaps nowhere is the promise of having the Lord's Spirit to be with us brought to our minds more forcefully and frequently than during the weekly sacramental service. In the blessing on the bread we are told that in order for us to *always* have *his Spirit to be with us*, we are to *do* certain things. In other words, like in so many things associated with the gospel, action is required on our part. When partaking of the bread we bear witness that we are willing to take upon us the name of Christ, always remember him, and keep his commandments. (See D&C 20:77.)

As we partake of the water, we bear witness that we "do always remember him." (D&C 20:79.) The importance of remembering Christ in order to have his Spirit was also emphasized when Christ instituted the sacrament prior to his crucifixion. (See JST Matthew 26:22.) These scriptures suggest that partaking of the sacrament is one of the most important things we can do to bring us closer to the Spirit.

To the Nephites, Christ said, "And if ye do always *remember me* ye shall have *my Spirit to be with you.*" (3 Nephi 18:11.) Remembering Christ is critical to being in tune with his Spirit. How do we remember him? We can begin remembering him when we pray. We might remember how he endured pain and sorrow and afflictions; how he responded with meekness when unjustly accused; how he always sought to do the will of his Father; how he showed love to others; and how he taught important principles to the people. We might seek to remember him by using the knowledge we have about him as a guide for our own lives. In whatever situation or circumstance we encounter, we might ask: "How would Christ handle this?" "What would he say if he were here?" "What can I do to pattern my life after his?"

In all that we do, it is important to *remember* his promise to us — that as we *remember* him we will *have his Spirit to be with us.*

Being in tune with the Spirit also requires that we live in such a way that the Spirit *can* be with us. It requires that we believe that such a power is available to us and that we are trying to live the best we know how.

We know that the Spirit of the Lord withdraws when there is "wickedness and hardness" of hearts. However, when we begin to "grow exceedingly in the knowledge of [our] God; . . . keep his statutes and commandments, and . . . walk in truth and uprightness before him," the Lord will pour out his Spirit upon us. (Helaman 6:34–36.) Elder Neal A. Maxwell writes, "[We] cannot have the influence of the Spirit if our lives do not reflect reasonable righteousness. We should, therefore, using the criteria given by the Lord, want to avoid trying to cover up our sins, gratifying our pride and advancing our vain ambitions, or exercising compulsion over others. We should want to live in such a way that our way of living reflects relationships with others that are filled with 'persuasion, long-suffering, gentleness, meekness, love unfeigned, kindness and pure knowledge' (D&C 121:36–41)." (*All These Things Shall Give Thee Experience* [Salt Lake City: Deseret Book], page 95.)

Shortly after joining the Church, I began to question my decision. Some professional friends suggested I'd been brainwashed; another wrote that the "Mormons wouldn't accept you in your alien religion" and suggested I had been pressured into joining the Church. Finally, I went to the man who had baptized me. I said, "This is the worst decision I've ever made in my life. I've been happy my whole life, and now I'm absolutely miserable."

He looked at me and simply asked, "What are you *not* doing that prevents you from having the Spirit of the Lord with you?" What was I *not* doing? "Nothing," I said. "I'm not doing anything." He said, "That's what I thought. You're not praying?" "No." "You're not reading the scriptures?" "No."

He admonished me. I went home and, for the first time in more than a month, prayed. I began again to read the Book of Mormon. And those things began to make all the difference.

73

The Fruits of the Spirit

In addition to learning about how the Spirit of the Lord can be recognized and what we might do to be more in tune with that Spirit, it is important for us to know *how* the Spirit of the Lord can influence us. Paul wrote to the Galatians and contrasted the "works of the flesh" with the "fruit of the Spirit." The contrast is striking. He identified as works of the flesh the following: adultery, fornication, uncleanness, lasciviousness, idolatry, witchcraft, hatred, variance, emulations, wrath, strife, seditions, heresies, envyings, murders, drunkenness, and revellings.

In contrast, the fruits of the Spirit include "love, joy, peace, longsuffering, gentleness, goodness, faith, meekness [and] temperance." No wonder Paul advised us to "walk in the Spirit." (See Galatians 5:16–23.) Repeatedly, scriptures in the Book of Mormon tell us that the influence of the Spirit of the Lord in our lives encourages us to do good:

"Because of the Spirit of the Lord Omnipotent, which has wrought a mighty change in us, or in our hearts . . . we have no more disposition to do evil, but to do good continually." (Mosiah 5:2.)

"That which is of God inviteth and enticeth to do good continually; wherefore, every thing which inviteth and enticeth to do good, and to love God, and to serve him, is inspired of God. . . . The Spirit of Christ is given to every man, that he may know good from evil." (Moroni 7:13, 16.)

"And by the power of the Holy Ghost ye may know the truth of all things. And whatsoever thing is good and just and true; wherefore, nothing that is good denieth the Christ, but acknowledgeth that he is." (Moroni 10:6.)

"Put your trust in that Spirit which leadeth to do good — yea, to do justly, to walk humbly, to judge righteously; and this is my Spirit." (D&C 11:12.)

One morning when I was feeling like I was just "not on track," I prayed to better know what I might do to be and do better. At lunch time, instead of eating, I chose to spend some time alone. I felt impressed to write the following ideas that came to my mind:

1. Acknowledgment:
    - My nothingness—dependence on Him (Mosiah 2:20–21).
    - God is omnipotent (1 Nephi 9:6) and omniscient (Helaman 9:41).
    - He knows, cares about, loves me personally (1 Nephi 11:17);
    - He has sent angels to guard me (D&C 84:88).

2. What does he want me to do?
    - Learn from scriptures, pray, seek the guidance of the Holy Ghost (2 Nephi 32:3, 5, 8, 9).
    - Learn to know His will and carry it out (John 5:30).
    - Understand that His will is more important than my will (Mark 3:35).
    - Learn the importance of His work, and that it is more important than my work. (John 8:28–29).
    - Understand that His work is saving souls (D&C 18:15).
    - Work to bring immortality and eternal life to others (Moses 1:39).

3. What do I need to do to prepare to do his will?
    - Put off the natural man; become a saint (Mosiah 3:19).
    - Humble myself (Alma 13:28).
    - Call on His name.
    - Watch and pray to not be tempted.
    - Be led by the Holy Spirit.

Later, I realized that each thought reflected an idea I had read in the scriptures. I searched the scriptures and added the references to my lunch time "food for thought."

When the Spirit Withdraws

Any discussion about being in tune with the Spirit of the Lord would be incomplete without acknowledging that there are times in our lives when the Spirit withdraws and we are left to our own judgment. I have come to believe that this is not necessarily due to unrighteous living or because we aren't doing certain things in our lives, but rather because there are times when, for the purpose of our own growth or experience, this is the will of our Heavenly Father.

The Prophet Joseph Smith cried out when he was imprisoned in Liberty Jail, "O God, where art thou? And where is the pavilion that covereth thy hiding place? How long shall thy hand be stayed, and thine eye, yea thy pure eye, behold from the eternal heavens the wrongs of thy people and of thy servants, and thine ear be penetrated with their cries?" (D&C 121:1–2.) Christ himself, hanging on the cross, pleaded, "My God, my God, why hast thou forsaken me?" (Matthew 27:46.)

Perhaps in such times of trial and tribulation we are expected to prove ourselves "true" even without the benefit of the influence of the Spirit. Our challenge is to be righteous at all times, under all conditions and circumstances.

Reflecting on this idea, and having experienced times when I felt very much alone and would question the strength of my faith or my humility or righteousness, I recorded the following in my journal:

> President Brigham Young once made a statement which impressed me very much. In a quiet moment with his secretary and two others, someone said, "President Young, why is it that the Lord is not always at our side

promoting universal happiness and seeing to it that the needs of people are met, caring especially for His Saints? Why is it so difficult at times?"

President Young answered, "Because man is destined to be a God, and he must be able to demonstrate that he is for God and to develop his own resources so that he can act independently and yet humbly." Then he added, "It is the way it is because we must learn to be righteous in the dark." (See Brigham Young's Office Journal, 28 January 1957.)

For me, learning to be "righteous in the dark" is part of my challenge in life. I have found times of spiritual abundance alternating with feelings of perceived abandonment. In pondering this idea one day, I wrote the following in my journal:

> Because of my experiences prior to joining the Church, I expected that following my baptism I would experience one big spiritual high. The passing years have taught me otherwise. Instead, I find that mountain-top experiences are separated by valleys, even deserts. I struggle with ambiguities and contradictions. I am disturbed by discrepancies between gospel principles and practices. Often I have more questions than answers, and, like Nephi, I often feel "encompassed about, because of the temptations and sins which do easily beset me." (2 Nephi 4:18.)
>
> However, after passing through spiritual deserts where I have struggled with problems, I gain new insights and understandings and realize how finite my own vision is. I no longer equate ease and comfort with happiness and contentment, but am in the process of coming to better understand the peace and joy spoken of in the gospel. No wonder our Heavenly Father, whose knowledge is perfect, provides us with spiritual valleys as well as spiritual peaks.

Whether we are in a spiritual valley or on a spiritual peak, the Lord is mindful of us. He has promised, "By this shall you know, all things whatsoever you desire of me, which are pertaining unto things of righteousness, in faith believing in me that you shall receive." (D&C 11:14.)

May we actively seek for and desire his Spirit. And in our tightly scheduled lives, may we pause to feel and sense his spirit of goodness and assurance. As we are in tune with the still, small voice, we will be gently guided and enabled to "go forth in the strength of the Lord."

Chapter Seven

Pray Always and Be Believing

From the time I was a young child I have believed in prayer. My parents taught me about it, I heard others pray, and it has always seemed like the right thing to do. I have heard many bear testimony that their prayers have been answered—that they have found their way when they have been lost, received guidance on an important decision, or found a way to relate to one of their children who seemed lost and alienated from the family. I also know people who feel frustrated and even guilty because they have prayed with all of their soul and yet have sensed no guidance on important matters. They begin to question their own faith, the "rightness" of their prayer, or even if God exists.

The scriptures are clear on our responsibilities concerning prayer. Repeatedly we are admonished to "pray always." (See 2 Nephi 32:9; Alma 13:28; 3 Nephi 18:18; D&C 10; D&C 88:126; Matthew 26:41; Mark 13:33; Luke 21:36.) The scriptures also contain numerous and repeated references to Christ, our Exemplar, praying to the Father. Likewise, the scriptures are filled with examples of others who prayed to God for a variety of reasons – to praise God, to express thanks, to seek for guidance, to be healed, to receive comfort, to resist temptation, to plead for forgiveness, to experience patience, to seek a blessing such as relief from drought, and so forth. Many people have written about prayer – how to pray, when to pray, the appropriate language of prayer, and how to prepare ourselves to pray.

For all I have come to know and experience about prayer, there have been times when I've still had many questions about this form of communication with our Father. Why is it that sometimes answers seem to come so clearly, almost before we've said the prayer, and yet at other times, after intensive and persistent pleadings with the Lord, we feel we are left on our own? Does receiving an answer one time and not another mean we pray with more faith sometimes? Does it mean that at times we are seeking the wrong, or an unrighteous, blessing?

Our Relationship to Heavenly Father

One day when earnestly seeking to better understand prayer and to make it more meaningful in my own life, I read the following statement in the Bible Dictionary: "As soon as we learn the true relationship in which we stand toward God (namely, God is our Father, and we are his children), then at once prayer becomes natural and instinctive on our part. Many of the so-called difficulties about prayer arise from forgetting this relationship." (LDS Edition of the King James Version, "Bible Dictionary," page 752.)

Suddenly my mind was flooded with thoughts. Although we cannot remember the time prior to our earthly birth, we do know that we are the spirit children of Heavenly Parents. We lived with them, were taught by them, and had opportunities to commune with them. If we were to become perfect, it was necessary for us to leave our Heavenly Father and our premortal home, and come to earth. When we were born of mortal parents, a veil covered our spiritual eyes and we could no longer remember our pre-earth experiences.

God endowed man with "agency." (Moses 7:32.) With this agency, man became free to choose "liberty and eternal life . . . or captivity and death." (2 Nephi 2:27.) We are to be "tried in all things" (D&C 136:31) to "see if [we] will do all things whatsoever the Lord [our] God shall command [us]." (Abraham 3:25.)

The plan was not that we would be sent to earth and left on our own. The first instruction the Lord gave Adam and Eve after they were driven from the Garden of Eden was to pray. (See Moses 5:5.) In other words, through prayer man, though physically separated from God, could continue to commune with him.

The desire of our Heavenly Father is for us to ultimately return to him. Anticipating the fall of Adam and Eve, God provided a Redeemer to rescue us from the Fall and to show us a perfect example of how to live so that we might become more godly. As I thought about this great plan of salvation, several things became very clear to me: I am *literally* a spirit child of my heavenly parents; I lived with them, I knew them, and they knew me well; to grow in wisdom and knowledge and judgment, it was necessary for me to leave my Heavenly Parents and come to earth and receive an earthly body; I was given agency—I can make choices and will learn from them; the plan is for me to ultimately return to my Heavenly Father; this is made possible through the Atonement of Christ. Through his life I can learn how to live my life. I have not been left here on the earth alone with no knowledge of who I am or why I am here. The scriptures teach me about these things. They also teach me about God and what he is like and of his concern for me.

Communicating with Our Father

As these thoughts came to my mind I began to more clearly understand the purpose of prayer. It is the means by which I have continued opportunities to call upon and talk with my Heavenly Father, now that I am no longer in his presence. Because I believe that he is all-knowing and that he knows me better than I know myself — as earthly parents often know their children better than the children know themselves — I know that he will respond to me in ways that are best for me.

When we come to understand that prayer is our means of access to God our Father, we become increasingly more comfortable in calling upon him. When we know that our Father knows us and hears us and responds to us, we will be anxious to "commune" with him. (See Exodus 25:22.) It is then that we will put aside "vain repetitions" (3 Nephi 13:7) and "pour out our whole souls to God." (Mosiah 28:14.) Ultimately, we will be more anxious to listen than to rehearse our own litany of lists.

How often, in the hope of fulfilling the responsibility we feel to pray, do we simply go through the motions of prayer? The following fictional dialogue causes us to think about Moroni's admonition to pray "with real intent of heart." (Moroni 6:9.)

> My Dear Father in Heaven . . .
> *Yes!*
> Don't interrupt me. I'm praying.
> *But you called me.*
> Called you? I didn't call you. I'm praying . . . My Dear Father in Heaven . . .
> *You did it again.*

Did what?

Called me. You said, "My dear Father in Heaven. Here I am. What do you have on your mind?

But I didn't mean anything by it. I was just saying my prayers for the night. I always say my prayers. It makes me feel good—like getting my duty done.

All right. Go on.

I'm thankful for my many blessings.

How thankful?

What?

How thankful are you for your "many blessings"?

I'm . . . well . . . I don't know. How should I know? It's just part of the prayer. Everyone always says we should express thanks.

All right. You're welcome. Go on.

Go on?

With your prayer.

Let's see. Bless the poor and the sick and the needy and the afflicted . . .

Do you really mean that?

Well, sure, I mean it.

What are you doing about it?

Doing? Who me? Nothing, I guess. I just think that it would be kind of nice if you got control of things down here like you have up there so people didn't have to suffer so much.

Have I got control of you?

Well, I go to Church. I pay my tithing. I don't smoke or drink.

That isn't what I asked you. What about your temper? You have a problem with your temper, and your friends and family suffer. There's also the way you spend your money—all on yourself. And what about the kind of books you read?

Stop picking on me! I'm just as good as some of the rest of those I see Sunday at Church.

But I thought you were praying for me to bless the

*needy. If that is to happen, I'll have to have help from
the ones who are praying for it—like you.*

Oh, all right. I guess I have a few hang-ups. Now that
you mention it, I could probably mention some others
too. But, look, I need to finish up here. This is taking a
lot longer than usual. Bless the missionaries to be led to
the doors of the honest in heart.

You mean people like Margaret?

Margaret?

Yes. The woman around the corner.

That Margaret? But she smokes and never goes to
church.

Have you had a look at her heart lately?

Of course not. How can . . .

*I've looked, and hers is one of those honest hearts that
you were just praying about.*

Well then, get the missionaries over there. Do you think
I like having a nonmember for a neighbor?

*You're supposed to be a missionary. Everyone is a mis-
sionary.*

Hey, wait a minute? What is this, "Criticize Me Day"?
Here I am, doing my duty, keeping your commandment
to pray; and all of a sudden, you break in and start re-
minding me of all of my problems.

*You called me. And here I am. Keep on praying. I'm
interested. Go on.*

I don't want to.

Why not?

I know what you'll say.

Go ahead.

Please forgive me of all my sins, and help me to forgive
others.

What about Bill?

See! I knew it! I knew you'd bring him up! Listen,
Father, he told lies about me, and I lost a job. Everyone
in that office thinks I'm a first-class creep, and I didn't
do anything. I'm going to get even with him.

But your prayers. What about your prayers?

I didn't mean it.

Do you enjoy carrying that load of bitterness around?

No, I don't. But I'll feel better as soon as I get even.

Do you want to know something?

What?

You won't feel better. You'll feel worse. Listen to me, you forgive Bill, and I'll forgive you.

But Father, I can't forgive Bill.

Then I can't forgive you.

No matter what?

No matter what. But you're not through with your prayer yet. Go on.

Please help me not to fall into temptation.

Good. I'll do that. But you stop putting yourself in all those places where you can be tempted.

What do you mean by that?

Stop hanging around the magazine racks and spending so much time in front of the TV. Some of that material will get to you sooner or later. You'll find yourself involved in some unfortunate things before long.

I don't understand.

Yes, you do. You find yourself in a crisis situation, and then you come running to me. "Father, help me out of this mess, and I promise I'll never do it again." It's amazing how the quality and intensity of your prayers improve when you are in trouble. Do you remember some of those bargains you've made with me?

Well, I don't think . . . Oh, yeah. Like the time Mom's visiting teacher saw me coming out of that movie about . . . Oh, brother!

Do you remember your prayer? I do. "Oh, Father. Don't let her tell my mother where I've been. I promise I'll go to nothing but G-rated movies from now on." She didn't tell your mother, but you didn't keep your promise. Did you?

No, Father, I didn't. I'm sorry.

So am I. Go ahead and finish your prayer.

Wait a minute. I want to ask you a question. Do you always listen to my prayers?

Every word. Every time.

Then how come you never talked back to me before?

How many chances have you given me? There's not enough time between your "amen" and your head hitting the pillow for me to draw a breath. How am I supposed to give an answer?

You could, if you really wanted to.

No. I could if you really wanted me to. I always want to.

Father, I'm sorry. Will you forgive me?

I already have. And thank you for letting me interrupt. I get lonely to talk to you sometimes. Good night. I love you.

Good night. I love you too.

(Used at Brigham Young University Education Week, August 1986. A similar presentation was used in a sacrament meeting in Bountiful, Utah, in July 1986. The author was unknown and I have since modified the script.)

A scripture concerning prayer which had always troubled me suddenly became understandable to me. ("The eyes of my understanding were opened"—D&C 138:11.) Christ said to his disciples: "Ask, and it shall be given unto you; seek, and ye shall find; knock, and it shall be opened unto you." (Luke 11:9.) That instruction seems clear enough, but what follows gives us great insight concerning our Father in Heaven: "If a son shall ask bread of any of you that is a father, will he give him a stone? or if he ask a fish, will he for a fish give him a serpent? Or if he shall ask an egg, will he offer him a scorpion? If ye then, being evil, know how to give good gifts unto your children: how much more shall your heavenly Father give the Holy Spirit to them that ask him?" (Luke 11:11–13.)

These scriptures relate a father responding to a son to

our Heavenly Father responding to us. Often a child asks for something, but either because of experience or knowledge or understanding (of the child and/or the situation), the parent does not give the child what he asks for. This may occur because the request is not in the child's best interest, or because of the parent's love for the child. Sometimes in being given "bread" the child perceives he is really receiving "a stone."

I remember one occasion when I was babysitting my younger brother, who was about sixteen months old. He'd wandered out of my sight, and after several minutes of not hearing him I went to investigate. He had managed to climb up a chair and onto the cupboard. There he sat, as proud as he could be of his accomplishment, happily playing with a shiny and very sharp butcher knife. Even though I was only twelve years old, I knew enough to take the knife away from him before he hurt himself. He immediately began to cry. He had been attracted to the knife because it was bright and shiny; to him, it was a plaything. But no matter how hard he cried, I would not give it to him. Now, some forty years later, I would not take a knife away from my brother. His own experience and judgment have matured to the point that he can handle a butcher knife without inflicting harm to himself.

Even though there were times I "thought I would die" if my parents did not grant me what I thought I had to have, I'm grateful for their wisdom in denying my request. Likewise, I can now see that many of the things for which I prayed at an earlier age would have been to my detriment or deprived me of growth if they had been granted the way I wanted and expected.

All of our prayers *are* answered, though sometimes not in the way we anticipate (and in retrospect, how grateful we can be that they are not).

Even the Savior's prayer in Gethsemane was answered in the negative. In addition to learning that prayers are not always answered as we wish them to be, we learn two other important lessons from the Savior's experience. First, following his prayer we are told that an angel appeared unto him, strengthening him. Sometimes when we wish for a certain situation to be resolved or made right or prevent it from happening, it is in our own best interest to be blessed instead with peace or understanding or additional knowledge or comfort or courage or increased faith or strength to bear up. Our Heavenly Father who is all-knowing, all-wise, and who loves us very much, will always answer our prayers!

Not My Will but Thine

The second thing we learn from Christ's prayer in Gethsemane is that he prayed, "Nevertheless not my will, but thine, be done." (Luke 22:42.) What a lesson for those of us who desire to be Christlike. Christ desired to do the Father's will. Even in the premortal life we have record of Christ, the Beloved Son, saying, "Father, thy will be done, and the glory be thine forever." (Moses 4:2.)

On numerous occasions Christ told us, "I seek not mine own will, but the will of the Father which hath sent me." (John 5:30; see also 3 Nephi 27:13; D&C 19:24.) He who exemplified by his life his desire to do the Father's will taught us, "Not every one that saith unto me, Lord, Lord, shall enter into the kingdom of heaven; but he that doeth the will of my Father which is in heaven." (Matthew 7:21; see also 3 Nephi 14:21.) Like Christ, other prophets have prayed, "Thy will, O Lord, be done, and not mine." (Jacob 7:14; Alma 14:13.)

Often it is shortsightedness that causes us to question if God hears our prayers, or to believe that our prayers are unanswered. We lack the perspective of our Heavenly Father.

Knowing only our mortal existence, we often fail to see things in an eternal perspective.

Following his address at the Sermon on the Mount (and the similar discourse given to the Nephites), the Savior taught the disciples how to pray and concluded by giving them an example that has come to be known as the Lord's prayer. (See Matthew 6 and 3 Nephi 13.) In both instances, the disciples were instructed to pray to their Father "who art in heaven" and to pray that "thy will be done in earth, as it is in heaven." (Matthew 6:9–10; 3 Nephi 9:10.)

In Christ's instructions concerning how we are to pray, he indicates that our "Father knoweth what things [we] have need of, before [we] ask him." (Matthew 6:8; 3 Nephi 13:8.) Why then do we pray at all? I believe it is because as we go through the process of using words to express ideas, we are forced to clarify our thinking and, in most instances, come to a new and clearer understanding.

In the early stages of work to achieve my doctoral degree, I had what I thought was a brilliant idea for a dissertation and was anxious to talk it over with my advisor. I made an appointment, arrived at her office at the appointed hour, and told her my purpose in coming. She asked to see my written proposal·and an outline of what research I wanted to do.

"I don't have anything in writing yet," I responded. She dismissed me from her office and told me she would be glad to talk with me when I had something in writing.

I perceived her actions to be inappropriate and cruel. Yet, in the days that followed I discovered, as I struggled to put my thoughts into words, that I had not carefully thought through what I wanted to do. In fact, as a result of this exercise, I determined on my own that my idea would not be appropriate for a dissertation.

Often it is as we commune with our Heavenly Father

through prayer that things become clear in our own minds. As we commune with him and seek to have his will done in our lives, we take time to reflect on the counsel and instruction he has already given us through the scriptures. In fact, Christ tells us that when "my words abide in you, ye shall ask what ye will, and it shall be done unto you." (John 15:7.)

The Lord told Nephi, son of Helaman, that because "thou . . . hast not sought thine own life, but has sought my will," whatever he asked would be done. Nephi knew the Lord's will and the Lord knew Nephi. He knew that Nephi would "not ask that which is contrary to my will." (Helaman 10:4–5.)

It is incumbent upon us to learn the will of the Father. Perhaps that is why Nephi told us to "feast upon the words of Christ; for behold, the words of Christ will tell you all things what ye should do." He also taught us that the Spirit can teach us to pray. (See 2 Nephi 32:3, 8.) This idea is reinforced in a revelation given through the Prophet Joseph Smith: "He that asketh in the Spirit asketh according to the will of God." (D&C 46:30.) Likewise, the Spirit helps us to pray. Paul taught, "We know not what we should pray for as we ought: but the Spirit itself maketh intercession for us with groanings which cannot be uttered." (Romans 8:26.)

Study It Out in Your Mind

In our desire to respond to the invitation to "ask," we need also to be mindful of the Lord's admonition to Oliver Cowdery. "You have not understood," the Lord said. "You have supposed that I would give it unto you, when you took no thought save it was to ask me." The Lord then explains that Oliver needed first to "study it out in his mind." (D&C 9:7–8.) In my own experience, whether in writing or preparing a talk or trying to solve a problem, I have found

President Spencer W. Kimball's statement to be true: "Perspiration must precede inspiration; there must be effort before there is excellence. We must do more than pray for . . . outcomes, though we must surely pray. We must take thought. We must make effort. We must be patient. We must be spiritual." (Spencer W. Kimball, *The Teachings of Spencer W. Kimball* [Salt Lake City: Bookcraft, 1982], page 402.)

In many instances it is the *process* of searching and studying and struggling that becomes more beneficial than the answer itself. I had such an experience in responding as a member of the Young Women General Board to an assignment given by the Young Women General Presidency. Each board member was asked to give written expression to the Young Women logo. It was suggested that our thoughts be limited to one or two short paragraphs.

I was excited about the assignment and immediately thought of the torch representing the Light of Christ, of the need for young women to be "a light" in a dark world, and of the torch as a symbol for young women to become literal "standard bearers." I jotted down a list of ideas and words to serve as a springboard for my writing.

I awoke early the next Saturday morning, excited about putting my thoughts on paper. When I sat down to write, I felt impressed to go to the library. I looked up books under the words *torch* and *torch bearer* and was surprised by the variety of books related to these two words. I selected nearly thirty books from which I drew ideas and spent about four hours reading and making notes of phrases and words. Later, I reviewed scriptural references on light.

By early evening I finally felt prepared to write. I cleared everything off my desk and sat before a blank piece of paper. That's when the struggle began. Several hours later I had written only two paragraphs, which I didn't feel particularly good about. But the next morning when I awoke, many of the words I had written came to my mind in rhyme. I finally got up and read again a talk President Ezra Taft Benson had given to the young women of the Church and an article by Young Women General President Ardeth G. Kapp in which she had called on young women to "stand up and lead out."

I then wrote the following:

Young women of these latter days, reserved till now for birth,
Your sacred mission was ordained before you came to earth.
In times when people everywhere are searching for the truth,
They'll turn to you; will you step forth, O valiant, noble youth?
A special call has come to you: "Be strong; stand up; lead out.
Renew commitment; stand for truth; with faith you need not
*   doubt."*
A mighty wave is forming; it will move across the earth.
Come, join the wave of truth and light, O youth of royal birth.
Young women of these latter days, we'll hold our torches high,
That Christ's true light through us will shine, his name to
*   glorify.*

I hear the call. I want to serve. The mighty wave I see.
I will stand up for all that's right. I will, O Lord; send me.
Our values help us as we seek to know and live the truth.
With willing hearts and minds we'll serve while we are in our
*   youth.*
With torches high and burning bright, we'll seek to light the
*   way,*
That all might find the narrow path and eagerly obey.

We will awake, arise, shine forth, and standard bearers be.
With all our strength, with all our love, Christ's witnesses we'll
*   be.*
Young women of these latter days, we'll hold our torches high,
That Christ's true light through us will shine, his name to
*   glorify.*

I had never written anything like this before and possibly

will not again. What I wrote came after study and struggle. I had completed the assignment. I had done the best I knew how. Ultimately, the Lord used my preparation and work to fulfill a purpose I could not have foreseen. The words I wrote were later put to music and used to introduce the Young Women's logo in a satellite broadcast.

We must learn that the immediacy of an answer to our prayers, or the perceived "no answer," is always given in our best interests. A loving Heavenly Father responds to his children in ways that are best for them and for their growth. The scriptures tell us that he will give us that thing "which is right" (3 Nephi 18:19) and "that is expedient for [us]" (D&C 88:64).

I have always been touched by the story of Amanda Smith. This incident took place following the massacre at Haun's Mill in October 1838. Many had been brutally killed, but Amanda survived and returned to the scene in search of her husband and three sons. From a distance she saw one of her older sons carrying a younger brother and she cried out, "Oh! My Alma is dead!" Her son replied, "No, mother, I think Alma is not dead. But father and brother Sardius are killed." Later Amanda was to record in her journal:

> What an answer was this to appal (sic) me! My husband and son murdered; another little son seemingly mortally wounded; and perhaps before the dreadful night should pass the murderers would return and complete their work!
>
> But I could not weep then. The fountain of tears was dry; the heart overburdened with its calamity, and all the mother's sense absorbed in its anxiety for the precious boy which God alone could save by his miraculous aid.
>
> The entire hip joint of my wounded boy had been shot away. Flesh, hip bone, joint and all had been ploughed out from the muzzle of the gun which the ruffian placed

to the child's hip through the logs of the shop and deliberately fired.

We laid little Alma on a bed in our tent and I examined the wound. It was a ghastly sight. I knew not what to do. It was night now. . . .

The women were sobbing, in the greatest anguish of spirit; the children were crying loudly with fear and grief at the loss of fathers and brothers; the dogs howled over their dead masters and the cattle were terrified with the scent of the blood of the murdered.

Yet was I there, all that long, dreadful night, with my dead and my wounded, and none but God as our physician and help. (Edward W. Tullidge, *The Women of Mormondom* [New York: Tullidge and Crandall, 1877], pages 122–128.)

Amanda, in her anguish, cried to her Heavenly Father as might a child in trouble cry to her earthly father. Her cry for help was simple, short, and to the point. From her faithful, believing heart she cried, "Oh my Heavenly Father, what shall I do? Thou seest my poor wounded boy and knowest my inexperience. Oh Heavenly Father, direct me what to do!" Immediately she received an answer and was directed as if by a voice.

Nearby was a slippery-elm tree. From this I was told to make a slippery-elm poultice and fill the wound with it. . . . I removed the wounded boy to a house, some distance off the next day, and dressed his hip; the Lord directing me as before. I was reminded that in my husband's trunk there was a bottle of balsam. This I poured into the wound, greatly soothing Alma's pain. . . .

So Alma laid on his face for five weeks, until he was entirely recovered — a flexible gristle having grown in place of the missing joint and socket, which remains to this day a marvel to physicians. (*The Women of Mormondom*, pages 122–128.)

There are many scriptures about prayer. All are instructive. They help us better understand prayer and how to pray and give us examples of those who prayed in a variety of situations and circumstances.

I sincerely believe that one of the "keys" to our prayers is to remember that we are praying to our Heavenly Father who loves us and wants the best for us. The more we become familiar with his power, his knowledge, and his ways, the more we will desire to seek to do his will.

Then whatever our challenge or adversity may be, we will receive from him all that is needed in order for us to "go forth in the strength of the Lord."

PART III
THE PROMISE

Chapter Eight

Come Unto Christ and Be Perfected in Him

To fully understand Christ's invitation to come unto him, we must start at the beginning—with Adam and Eve.

After Adam and Eve ate of the forbidden fruit, they were driven out of the Garden of Eden. Although they were shut out from the presence of God, they called upon him and he spoke to them. Then God gave Adam and Eve two commandments: to worship the Lord their God, and to offer up by way of sacrifice the firstlings of their flocks. Many days later an angel appeared to Adam asking him why he offered sacrifices to the Lord. He replied simply, "I know not, save the Lord commanded me." Adam was then told by the angel that such sacrifices were in the "similitude of the sacrifice of the Only Begotten of the Father, which is full of grace and truth." Then Adam and Eve were told to do everything in "the name of the Son" and to repent and to call upon God in the name of the Son forever. (See Moses 5:5–8.)

On that day, the Holy Ghost fell upon Adam and Eve

and bore record of the Father and the Son, telling him that through Christ he and all mankind could be redeemed from the Fall. When Adam heard these things, he blessed God and began to prophesy to "all the families of the earth, saying, Blessed be the name of God, for because of my transgression my eyes are opened, and in this life I shall have joy, and again in the flesh I shall see God." (Moses 5:10.)

What Adam proclaimed to "all families" and to each of us is the "good news" of the gospel—that because of Jesus Christ we can be saved. He is the reason for our joy and the basis for our faith.

Our salvation and joy, like Adam and Eve's, is made possible by the atoning sacrifice of God's son, Jesus Christ. Christ is for us, as he was for Adam and Eve, a literal Savior: He and he alone can *save* us from our sins.

But what does this "good news" have to do with the instruction from God that Adam and Eve should offer the "firstlings of their flocks" as an offering? Such an offering was to remind them of the sacrifice which the Son of God would make for the sins of the world. The firstling of the flock was to be the best, the one without spot or blemish, perfect in every way. This sacrifice was to typify that, as the lamb "before her shearers is dumb" (Isaiah 53:7), so Christ, when falsely accused by the chief priests, "answered nothing." (Mark 15:3–5.)

And so from the day of Adam and Eve through many generations, the offering of sacrifices was practiced by the people. Under the law of Moses sacrifices became varied and complex, but the purpose of the sacrifice was always the same—to cause the people to *"look forward with stead-fastness unto Christ"* (2 Nephi 25:24), and to "keep them *in remembrance of God* and their duty towards him." (Mosiah 13:30.)

In our day we, too, need to be kept in remembrance of God and reminded of our duty to him. We are repeatedly commanded to pray unto the Father through Christ and to keep his commandments. It is through study of the scriptures that we can be brought to a *remembrance* of the great and marvelous works of God to people of all ages. It is for this same purpose that we are commanded to "meet together often to partake of bread and wine *in the remembrance* of the Lord Jesus." (D&C 20:75.) Christ taught the Nephites that the sacrament "shall be a testimony unto the Father that ye do always *remember me.*" (3 Nephi 18:7.)

But no longer do we offer the firstling of the flock as required of Adam and Eve. Amulek taught the people the doctrine of the Atonement, explaining that it was necessary "that there should be a great and last sacrifice . . . to stop the shedding of blood" and to fulfill the law of Moses. This "great and last sacrifice will be the Son of God. . . . And thus he shall bring salvation to all those who shall believe on his name." (Alma 34:13–15.)

Jesus Christ, the Firstborn of the Father, the Perfect One, has fulfilled the law which required the offering of the firstling of the flock. Following his resurrection, Christ himself told the Nephites, "In me is the law of Moses fulfilled. . . . Your sacrifices and your burnt offerings shall be done away." (3 Nephi 9:17, 19.)

A Broken Heart and a Contrite Spirit

Because the law of Moses has been fulfilled, we no longer offer animal sacrifices. Instead, we are to offer for a sacrifice to Christ a *"broken heart and a contrite spirit"* (3 Nephi 9:20; 12:18–19) — a heart that aches as we think about how inconsiderate we were to someone, or how impatiently we responded to the clerk at the store, or the unkind things we said about our neighbor. Our hearts begin to break as we realize that we are often filled with envy and jealously and pride. We are pained when we think of simple things we might have done to lift another's burden, or of times when we could have so easily spoken an encouraging word but did not. Perhaps we've cheated or lied or been dishonest in a dozen other ways that seemed so innocent at the time. Maybe we've committed a moral transgression or been involved with the misuse of drugs.

For each of us there will come a day when we wish we'd done things better, or when we realize that there is no way we can make everything right. If justice were demanded — if we had to pay a penalty for everything we've done wrong or for good things we failed to do — we simply could not do it. We could not pay the debt. But the debt has already been paid. Christ's death on the cross, "the great and last sacrifice," was to "bring about the bowels of mercy, which overpowereth justice; . . . mercy can satisfy the demands of justice." (Alma 34:15–16.)

For our sacrifice we are to offer "a broken heart and a contrite spirit"; to admit that we're sorry for our wrongdoings and that we want to do better. We acknowledge that we need Christ.

That is the key — to recognize that we need him. Until we come to that point in our lives, he will simply "stand at the door, and knock." But when we come to know that we need him and subsequently invite him into our lives, "He will come in and sup with us." (Revelation 3:20.)

Experience a Mighty Change

Once we invite Christ into our lives, we will experience "a mighty change." (See Mosiah 5:2; Alma 5:26.) Through the ages many people have heard the message of Christ and invited him into their lives; and because of his mercy and love, their lives have been changed.

Saul of Tarsus was actively involved in persecuting the Christians until he saw a vision on the road to Damascus. Because of Christ, Saul had both his heart and his name changed, and he spent the rest of his life in the service of his new master.

A young girl might have lived her life as a humble, obscure woman in the village of Nazareth, but following a visit from an angel she committed to serve as "handmaiden of the Lord" and became the earthly mother of Jesus. (See Luke 1:38.)

A nameless woman from Samaria responded to Christ's request for a drink of water, and after learning of a "well of water springing up into everlasting life" she left her waterpot and became a missionary for Christ. (See John 4:5–30.)

Mary called Magdalene felt Christ's healing influence as he rebuked from her seven devils. Her complete devotion to Christ was evidenced as she was one among the women last at the cross and first at the tomb. (See Luke 8:2; Matthew 27:56, 61.)

Because the Lamanites and Nephites believed and lived Christ's teachings "the love of God did dwell in the hearts of the people," and they were able to live without contentions or disputations — "they had all things in common and there could not be a happier people." (See 4 Nephi 1:2, 3, 15, 16.)

The multitudes who heard King Benjamin bear testimony that through the atonement of Christ people could put off the natural man and become saints had a "mighty change" wrought in their hearts and were called the "children of Christ." (See Mosiah 4:17, 19; 5:2, 7.)

The Nephite babes and children who were blessed and taught and ministered unto by Christ had their tongues loosed and "did speak unto their fathers great and marvelous things, even greater than he had revealed unto the people." (3 Nephi 7:21; 26:14–16.)

In the final chapters of the Book of Mormon, every Nephite who would not deny Christ was put to death. But Moroni could not deny his Savior. He had seen his father and all of his kinsfolk slain in battle; he had no friends. And though the whole face of the land was "one continual round of murder and bloodshed," he spent the remainder of his days preparing a record for our day. In that record he posed to each of us the question, "Why are ye ashamed to take upon you the name of Christ?" (Mormon 8:5, 8, 35, 38; Moroni 1:1–3.)

The men and women and children who invited Christ into their lives and who accepted him were changed by him. They did not live lives free from hardship or illness or sorrow or loneliness. Among them were those who were rejected by their friends and others, stoned, persecuted, and imprisoned; many lost their earthly possessions and suffered death because of their belief in Christ.

Without exception, even in the midst of great trials and tribulation, these people of Christ spoke about experiencing peace, comfort, success, joy (exceeding and exquisite), courage, strength beyond their own, happiness, patience, fellowship, confidence, wisdom, and power. Like Moses, they chose "to suffer affliction with the people of God, than to enjoy the pleasures of sin for a season." (Hebrews 11:25.)

And there were many who were willing to give away their worldly wealth (large or small) to receive the gifts and blessings promised by Christ. Zacchaeus, a rich man who was chief among the Publicans, came down from a sycamore tree, received Christ "joyfully," and restored fourfold anything he had taken from a man by false accusation. (See Luke 19:1–9.)

Simon and his brother Andrew "forsook their nets, and

followed him." (Mark 1:18.) Mary, sister of Martha, left some things undone and chose the "good part"—the one needful thing that could not be taken away from her. (Luke 10:38–42.) Upon hearing about the atonement of Christ and hope of the Resurrection, the father of King Lamoni said, "I will give up all that I possess, yea, I will forsake my kingdom. . . . I will give away all my sins to know [God]." (Alma 22:15, 18.)

Will you accept the invitation of the Savior? He stands at the door and knocks, waiting for our response. "Come," he says, "and fear not, and lay aside every sin, which easily doth beset you, which doth bind you down . . . come and go forth, and show unto your God that ye are willing to repent of your sins and enter into a covenant with him to keep his commandments." (Alma 7:15.)

Invite Christ into Your Life

All the Savior asks of us is that we repent—to lay aside our sins and to turn our heart and will to God; to do the things which Christ has done and to desire the things which he desired. Inviting Christ into our lives means bearing one another's burdens, mourning with those that mourn, comforting those who stand in need of comfort. (Mosiah 18:8–9.) It means making time to "succor the weak, lift up the hands which hang down, and strengthen the feeble knees." (D&C 81:5.)

President Ezra Taft Benson has said, "When you choose to follow Christ, you choose to be changed." ("Born of God," *Ensign*, November 1985, page 5.) C.S. Lewis borrows a parable from George MacDonald:

"Imagine yourself as a living house. God comes in to rebuild that house. At first, perhaps, you can understand what he is doing. He is getting the drains right and stopping the leaks in the roof and so on: you knew that those jobs needed doing and so you are not surprised. But presently he starts knocking the house about in a way that hurts abominably and does not seem to make sense. What on earth is He up to? The explanation is that He is building quite a different house from the one you thought of — throwing out a new wing here, putting on an extra floor there, running up towers, making courtyards. You thought you were going to be made into a decent little cottage; but He is building a palace. He intends to come and live in it Himself." (C.S. Lewis, *Mere Christianity*, Macmillan Publishing Co., Inc., page 174.)

The plan is for us to become perfect — perfect as are Christ and our Father in Heaven. But becoming perfect is as much a *process* as an end result. Just as Christ "received not of the fulness at first, but continued from grace to grace, until he received a fulness," so it is with us. (D&C 93:13.) The Prophet Joseph Smith compared the process of perfection to a ladder. We begin by climbing from the bottom, and we ascend to the top by taking one step at a time. (See *Teachings of the Prophet Joseph Smith*, page 348.)

And so it is with our faith. Few of us have the faith of Melchizedek to "break mountains, to divide the seas, [or] to dry up the waters, [and] to turn them out of their course." (JST Genesis 14:30.) Few of us can make "the very trees obey us, or the mountains, or the waves of the sea," as did Jacob. (Jacob 4:6.) Few there are among us who have the faith of Alma and Amulek to cause the prison to tumble to the earth. (See Ether 12:13; Alma 14:27.)

But we can "desire to believe" (Alma 32:27) and begin to "exercise faith in Christ; and . . . lay hold on every good thing." (Moroni 7:25.) We can "search the scriptures" (John 5:39), and "pray always and be believing." (D&C 90:24.) As we accept the invitation to "come unto Christ," he will enter into our hearts and into our minds through the promptings of the Spirit. As we seek to remember him, his words will come into our minds; we will begin to think of the things he would do; and we will have an increased desire to become like him and to respond as he would respond.

Go Forth in the Strength of the Lord

Like people of all ages, however, we must realize that having faith in Christ does not mean that challenges and hard times will go away. Pain will continue to exist, accidents will occur, and pollution of air and body and mind will not cease. Having faith in Christ does not mean that we will escape those who lie and cheat to get gain, devalue and make a mockery of life, take advantage of others, or scoff at prophets and visions and traditions. Having faith in Christ does not mean that there will not be times when there seems to be no virtue in righteousness, when it seems that obedience is for fools, or when it appears that lying and cheating bring reward. Having faith in Christ does not mean that we will see a decrease in our personal and family problems, become wealthy in terms of the standards of the world, or that our lives will become less complex.

Having faith in Jesus Christ *does mean* that we need never face any problem or challenge or trial or temptation alone. Having faith in Christ means that through his bounteous mercy and love we do have access to a divine means of help and strength—a power that will enable us to face every situation. Most importantly, faith in our Savior, Jesus Christ, will enable us to obtain a remittance of our sins and eventually return to the presence of God.

The first step on the ladder of increasing our faith is to believe and act upon the promises we find in Holy Writ:

"Be strong and of a good courage; be not afraid, neither be thou dismayed: for the Lord thy God is with thee whithersoever thou goest." (Joshua 1:9.)

"Treasure up [my] words in thy heart. Be faithful and diligent in keeping the commandments of God, and I will encircle thee in the arms of my love." (D&C 6:20.)

"For with God nothing shall be impossible." (Luke 1:37.)

"I will instruct thee and teach thee in the way which thou shalt go: I will guide thee with mine eye." (Psalm 32:8.)

"Ask the Father in the name of Jesus for what things soever ye shall stand in need. Doubt not, but be believing . . . and come unto the Lord with all your heart." (Mormon 9:27.)

"He giveth power to the faint; and to them that have no might he increaseth strength." (Isaiah 40:29.)

"My grace is sufficient for all men that humble themselves before me; for if they humble themselves before me, and have faith in me, then will I make weak things strong unto them." (Ether 12:27.)

"Look unto me in every thought; doubt not, fear not. Behold the wounds which pierced my side, and also the prints of the nails in my hands and feet; be faithful, keep my commandments, and ye shall inherit the kingdom of heaven." (D&C 6:36–37.)

"Yea, come unto Christ, and be perfected in him . . . and if ye shall deny yourselves of all ungodliness, and love God with all your might, mind and strength, then is his grace sufficient for you, that by his grace ye may be perfect in Christ." (Moroni 10:32.)

Believing and acting upon these promises will enable us not only to "go forth in the strength of the Lord," but to declare with the Apostle Paul, "I can do all things through Christ which strengtheneth me." (Philippians 4:13.)

Appendix

I have compiled a few of the scriptures I turn to at various times for various reasons. These are those scriptures that have had tremendous impact upon my life. May they provide evidence of the "powerful effect" which the word can have upon our minds.

When I Question My Abilities:

"And Christ hath said: If ye will have faith in me ye shall have power to do whatsoever thing is expedient in me." (Moroni 7:33.)

"And it shall come to pass that power shall rest upon thee; thou shalt have great faith, and I will be with thee and go before thy face." (D&C 39:12.)

"I am well pleased with your offering and acknowledgments, which you have made; for unto this end have I raised you up, that I might show forth my wisdom through the weak things of the earth." (D&C 124:1.)

"Therefore, let the morrow take thought for the things

of itself. Neither take ye thought beforehand what ye shall say; but treasure up in your minds continually the words of life, and it shall be given you in the very hour that portion that shall be meted unto every man." (D&C 84:84–85.)

"Behold, I do not condemn you; go your ways and sin no more; perform with soberness the work which I have commanded you." (D&C 6:35.)

"I will impart unto you of my Spirit, which shall enlighten your mind, which shall fill your soul with joy; And then shall ye know . . . all things whatsoever you desire of me, which are pertaining unto things of righteousness, in faith believing in me that you shall receive." (D&C 11:13–14.)

"Without faith you can do nothing; therefore ask in faith." (D&C 8:10.)

"But the Lord knoweth all things from the beginning; wherefore, he prepareth a way to accomplish all his works among the children of men; for behold, he hath all power unto the fulfilling of all his words." (1 Nephi 9:6.)

When I Am Worried about an Assignment:

"Behold, I will go before you and be your rearward; and I will be in your midst, and you shall not be confounded." (D&C 49:27.)

"Speak the thoughts that I shall put into your hearts, and you shall not be confounded before men; For it shall be given you in the very hour, yea, in the very moment, what ye shall say. . . . Declare whatsoever thing ye declare in my name, in solemnity of heart, in the spirit of meekness, in all things. And I give unto you this promise, that inasmuch as ye do this the Holy Ghost shall be shed forth in bearing record unto all things whatsover ye shall say." (D&C 100:5–8.)

"Be thou humble; and the Lord thy God shall lead thee by the hand, and give thee answer to thy prayers." (D&C 112:10.)

"And we ask thee, Holy Father, that thy servants may go forth from this house armed with thy power, and that thy name may be upon them, and thy glory be round about them, and thine angels have charge over them." (D&C 109:22.)

"Behold my Spirit is upon you, wherefore all thy words will I justify; and the mountains shall flee before you, and the rivers shall turn from their course; and thou shalt abide in me, and I in you; therefore walk with me." (Moses 6:34.)

When I Am Rushing and Need to Slow Down:

"Stand thou still a while, that I may shew thee the word of God." (1 Samuel 9:27.)

"Commune with your own heart upon your bed, and be still." (Psalm 4:4.)

"Be still, and know that I am God." (Psalm 46:10.)

"In quietness and in confidence shall be your strength." (Isaiah 30:15.)

"To every thing there is a season, and a time to every purpose under the heaven. . . . A time to keep silence, and a time to speak." (Ecclesiastes 3:1, 7.)

"Better is an handful with quietness, than both the hands full with travail and vexation of spirit." (Ecclesiastes 4:6.)

"Fear ye not, stand still, and see the salvation of the Lord." (Exodus 14:13.)

When I Am in Need of Comfort:

"Look unto God with firmness of mind, and pray unto him with exceeding faith, and he will console you in your afflictions, and he will plead your cause. . . . O all ye that are pure in heart, lift up your heads and receive the pleasing word of God, and feast upon his love." (Jacob 3:1–2.)

"And he shall go forth, suffering pains and afflictions and temptations of every kind; and this that the word might be fulfilled which saith he will take upon him the pains and the sicknesses of his people. And he will take upon him death, that he may loose the bands of death which bind his people; and he will take upon him their infirmities, that his bowels may be filled with mercy, according to the flesh, that he may know according to the flesh how to succor his people according to their infirmities." (Alma 7:11–12.)

"Listen to him who is the advocate with the Father, who is pleading your cause before him." (D&C 45:3.)

"I am the first and the last; I am he who liveth, I am he who was slain; I am your advocate with the Father." (D&C 110:4.)

When I Want to Remember Christ's Great Sacrifice for Me:

"And lo, he shall suffer temptations, and pain of body, hunger, thirst, and fatigue, even more than man can suffer, except it be unto death; for behold, blood cometh from every pore, so great shall be his anguish for the wickedness and the abominations of his people." (Mosiah 3:7.)

"For behold, I, God, have suffered these things for all, that they might not suffer if they would repent; But if they would not repent they must suffer even as I; Which suffering caused myself, even God, the greatest of all, to tremble because of pain, and to bleed at every pore, and to suffer both body and spirit — and would that I might not drink the bitter cup, and shrink." (D&C 19:16–18.)

"Then released he Barabbas unto them: and when he had scourged Jesus, he delivered him to be crucified. Then the soldiers of the governor took Jesus into the common hall, and gathered unto him the whole band of soldiers. And they stripped him, and put on him a scarlet robe. And when they had platted a crown of thorns, they put it upon his head, and a reed in his right hand: and they bowed the knee before him, and mocked him, saying, Hail, King of the Jews! And they spit upon him, and took the reed, and smote him on the head. And after that they had mocked him, they took the robe off from him, and put his own raiment on him, and led him away to crucify him." (Matthew 27:26–31.)

"And with him they crucify two thieves; the one on his right hand, and the other on his left. And the scripture was fulfilled, which saith, And he was numbered with the transgressors. And they that passed by railed on him, wagging their heads, and saying, Ah, thou that destroyest the temple, and buildest it in three days, Save thyself, and come down from the cross. Likewise also the chief priests mocking said among themselves with the scribes, He saved others; himself he cannot save. Let Christ the King of Israel descend now from the cross, that we may see and believe. And they that were crucified with him reviled him." (Mark 15:27–32.)

When My Faith Needs Strengthening:

Hebrews 11 and Ether 12

"If ye will have faith in me ye shall have power to do whatsoever thing is expedient in me. And he hath said: Repent all ye ends of the earth, and come unto me, and be baptized in my name, and have faith in me, that ye may be saved. . . . Have angels ceased to appear unto the children of men? Or has he withheld the power of the Holy Ghost from them? . . . Behold I say unto you, Nay; for it is by faith that miracles are wrought; and it is by faith that angels appear and minister unto men; wherefore, if these things have ceased wo be unto the children of men, for it is because of unbelief, and all is vain." (Moroni 7:33–37.)

"Thus God has provided a means that man, through faith, might work mighty miracles; therefore he becometh a great benefit to his fellow beings." (Mosiah 8:18.)

"If ye have faith ye can do all things which are expedient unto me." (Moroni 10:23.)

"And as all have not faith, seek ye diligently and teach one another words of wisdom; yea, seek ye out of the best books words of wisdom, seek learning even by study and also by faith." (D&C 109:7.)

Index

Index